MW01504673

Consumer Guide To
Diamonds

Third Edition

How to spend your fortune without making a mistake.

Joseph Mirsky

Contents

Preface

– Are you going to spend a fortune for a Diamond?

– Are you afraid you'll make a mistake?

– Do you know what an ideal cut diamond is?

This book is aimed at people to whom these questions give pause. As a gemologist and the owner of a jewelry store the need for a book to guide the consumer in the purchase of diamonds has been apparent to me for some time. Judging by the number of pretty bad diamonds I see, brought in for cleaning, repairs, appraisals, etc., people are not going about looking for diamonds correctly. This book is intended to guide you in the purchase of this high-anxiety, esoteric product. No other merchandise is graded so stringently and with no other merchandise do subtle differences in quality carry such large differences in price.

People freeze up when looking for diamonds because they're about to spend a lot of money, because many diamonds, especially engagement rings, are emotional rite-of-passage purchases, ego and social pressure require that they get "a deal", and because they know, or quickly find out, that there's a lot of bewildering technical business with letters and numbers involved.

Consequently, people abandon the common-sense idea of simply looking with their eyes and their search for a diamond becomes intellectualized. The diamond grades become pigeonholes: they find the diamond that fits the pigeonholes they think they want and, if the price is right, that's the diamond.

But the object of the enterprise is to buy something beautiful, and beauty should be judged first by the eye, and then by the mind's eye. It doesn't take that much of a "trained eye" to pick a beautiful diamond. You can get the training you need in the process of shopping, with limitations, provided you go to a variety of stores and look at a number of diamonds.

The art of a book such as this is not to merely summarize information about diamonds but also to address the misperceptions and misinformation that underlie the considerable consumer anxiety about diamonds and to tease out the underlying psychology that leads to common mistakes and bad decisions consumers make.

With the market flooded with low quality diamond jewelry and a burgeoning of non-traditional and non-professional outlets for jewelry it is essential to educate consumers about diamonds for their sake and for the sake of the jewelry industry, lest the appetite for diamonds be blunted by unsavory fare.

The third edition of this book brings it up to date with the changes in the diamond market, especially the reorganization of DeBeers, the diamond monopoly, and the emergence of diamond cut (putting the correct angles on the facets of a diamond to maximize brilliance) to the forefront of diamond marketing.

The third edition also includes through-the-microscope pictures of diamonds, to illustrate the text and to show you what to look for and to what to look out for, and appendices explaining precious metals and gemology.

Joseph Mirsky
Pompton Lakes, NJ
May, 2003

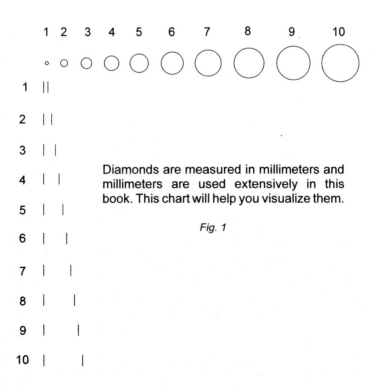

Diamonds are measured in millimeters and millimeters are used extensively in this book. This chart will help you visualize them.

Fig. 1

1. Fire and Ice — Birth of a Diamond

Some 75 to 120 miles below the great land masses, in the permanent cores of the wandering continents, the pressure and temperature are right to squeeze pure carbon from molten rock into extremely dense crystals of diamond.[1] Diamonds are then transported to the surface very rapidly by volcanoes, surviving the trip only if temperature in relation to pressure remains within narrow limits.

Now, don't run out to your neighborhood volcano and start digging. Diamonds only occur in specific types of volcanic rocks, kimberlites or lamproites, which are rare. Moreover, most of these rock deposits contain no diamonds. The most recent known deposition of diamonds was about 20 million years ago. The diamonds themselves are from 1 to 3 billion years old, much older than the transporting volcanic magma. (Diamonds themselves cannot be dated, but certain inclusions in them can be.) It is not known whether diamonds are being formed continuously, or only in some past epoch.

The cores of these volcanoes, eroded flat over the eons, are called pipes. The pipes become diamond mines. They range from about the size of a football field to ½ sq. mile.

The erosion of the soft rock washes some of the diamonds into stream beds to form alluvial deposits. These ancient streams may then be buried in sediment which is then transformed into rock. Sometimes diamonds are washed all the way to the sea, forming marine deposits. Alluvial and marine deposits are much richer in diamonds and in gem quality diamonds than the primary pipes. Diamonds and other heavy minerals settle out sooner and become concentrated. Highly strained or impure diamonds break up in the tumbling streams, leaving a higher concentration of gem quality diamonds.

India was the major source of diamonds from antiquity until their discovery in Brazil in the 1720's. These were all alluvial diamonds. The great diamond finds in South Africa in the 1870's were the first to tap into the primary diamond pipes and gave that country pre-eminence until recently. The vast quantities of diamonds from South African mines ushered in the modern era of diamonds for the masses.

---

1. Gem diamonds are 99.95% carbon, more pure than ivory soap. The atoms of diamond are more densely packed than any other solid, which accounts for its incomparable hardness.

Today, Australia is the largest producer of diamonds by weight, though not by value. The Argyle mine in the desert of northern Australia, the world's most prolific diamond mine, produces mainly small, low quality diamonds which are sent to India for low-wage cutting and wind up in mass-produced jewelry in the United States. The table below shows the main producers of the 110 million carats of gem and industrial diamonds mined in 2000. Over half of diamonds mined are industrial.

Principal Diamond Sources – 2000 Figures

Percent of World Production

By Weight		By Value	
Australia	23.4	Botswana	27.1
Botswana	22.4	Russia	21.6
Russia	18.7	South Africa	14.1
Congo	15.0	Congo	7.4
South Africa	9.6	Namibia	5.3
Namibia	1.5	Australia	4.6

As you can see from the chart above, Africa and Russia provide the bulk of better diamonds. There have been discoveries of diamond pipes in Canada, and the first Canadian mine, called the Ekati mine, opened in 1998, producing high quality diamonds. The Ekati mine now (2002) produces 6% of world diamond production, by value. Two more mines are scheduled to open and eventually Canada is expected to supply 10-15% of world diamond production.

Canadian diamonds are cut in Canada to high standards and are marketed as "clean" diamonds, as opposed to some African diamonds associated with human rights abuses and financing guerrilla warfare.

Canadian diamonds are laser-engraved on the edge with a logo (a polar bear, maple leaf, and other Canadian symbols – see photo p.84) and serial numbers, and come with certificates of origin. Some certificates even tell the weight of the rough diamond from which it was cut and where it was mined. One Canadian company even offers a pair of different size round diamonds cut from the same piece of rough accompanied by a photo of the rough.

Yes! There are diamond mines in the United States. There is a diamond mine at Kelsey Lake, Colorado which produces high quality diamonds. The production is small, though, and all the diamonds are sold within the state.

If you want to dig your own, you can! The Crater of Diamonds State Park in Murfreesboro, Arkansas will let you do it for a few bucks. Hand tools only. You can find out more information at www.state.ar.us.

Sorry, New Yorkers and New Jerseyans. Herkimer diamonds and Cape May diamonds aren't diamonds: they're quartz.

2. How Diamonds Are Cut

First you need to be familiar with a few terms. The basic parts of a diamond are the crown, table, girdle, pavilion, and culet.

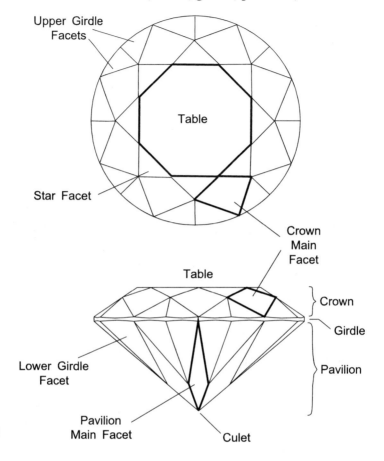

Upper Girdle Facets

Table

Star Facet

Crown Main Facet

Table

Crown

Girdle

Lower Girdle Facet

Pavilion

Fig. 2

Pavilion Main Facet

Culet

The crown is the top part of the diamond. The large horizontal stop sign shaped facet on the top of the crown is the table. The girdle is the edge, the widest part. The pavilion is the bottom part that slopes to the culet, or point, which may have a tiny flat facet (the 58th facet).

I'm sure you've seen cave-man movies (and, of course, a certain cartoon) which have people hunting dinosaurs or vice-versa. The fact that dinosaurs disappeared 65 million years before there were any people hasn't inconvenienced Hollywood at all. Likewise, if you see someone in a movie set in ancient or medieval times fondling a sparkling diamond, it's possible if he or she is of the nobility, although the diamond wouldn't have been very round or all that brilliant.

Diamonds were crudely fashioned by cleaving until about 1300. Subsequently, diamonds were laboriously hand-polished by rubbing against a board charged with diamond powder until the invention of the rotary lap, or scaife, around 1400. Diamonds so fashioned aren't very brilliant.

By the late 17th century what we now call the old mine cut had evolved. These diamonds were full cut brilliants (58 facets) although the cutting was crude by modern standards and they were squarish rather than round. A little later came the old European cut, which was round.

Fig. 3

Old Mine Diamond
This one is more asymmetrical than most. The black hole in the center is the large culet, which is typical. The black areas at the left are reflections of the culet due to the very steep crown.

Old European Cut
This diamond has the typical very small table and large culet. The facets have been outlined for clarity. There is a chip at the lower left.

The proportions of these modern precursors weren't correct for maximum brilliance and fire (the spreading of light by the stone into flashes of color). All the old cuts had a very large culet (a large flat on the bottom), which looks like a black hole in the center of the stone.

Modern diamond cutting begins with the invention of the rotary diamond saw around 1900. Before that the typical shape of diamond rough, two four-sided pyramids set base to base, called an octahedron, caused cutters to make diamonds with very high and steep crowns and with small tables, lest they grind away too much valuable diamond. With the advent of the saw, a typical rough diamond could be made into two diamonds with better proportions and with less waste.

In 1919, Marcel Tolkowsky, a member of a Belgian diamond cutting family and a mathematician, published as a masters thesis a mathematical analysis of the angles and proportions for a diamond design that would produce what he judged the best balance of brilliance and fire. These theoretical values were close to those evolved by trial and error by the best cutters as early as 1880.

Tolkowsky tested his theories by allowing the cutters of the diamond factory he managed to cut a large number of diamonds strictly for their own idea of beauty, regardless of waste. The proportions of these diamonds turned out to be very close to Tolkowsky's design. Tolkowsky's proportions came to be known as the ideal cut. They are only for round diamonds.

Tolkowky's treatise plus the increasing use of the diamond saw, which allowed his proportions to be cut economically, led to the ascendancy of the modern cut over the old mine and old European cuts in the 1920's. Unfortunately, it proved even more economical to cut diamonds with the opposite distortion to the old mine cuts, with shallow crowns and large tables, giving diamonds with unbalanced brilliance and little fire.

Diamonds are cut by first sawing the rough or dividing it by cleaving it along its natural atomic planes. Once the proper orientation in the crystal is determined, a groove is cut in the rough diamond. Traditionally, this was done by hand-rubbing another, specially pointed diamond, called a sharp, against it. Nowadays, lasers guided by computers are used to kerf diamonds with great precision. A blunt steel blade is then held in the groove and struck with a steel rod. Pressure against the walls of the groove initiates the cleavage, which shears the crystal along its natural atomic planes. This can be a heart-stopping moment with an important diamond, since a tiny misstep will shatter the diamond.

However most diamonds are divided by sawing. They are clamped in a holder and pressed against a very thin bronze disc whose edge is charged with diamond dust. The disc revolves at very high speed and cuts through the diamond. This can take hours, or even days when "naats", areas of distorted crystal formation, are encountered. Diamonds are also sawn by lasers.

Next the diamond is shaped in outline by chucking it in a lathe and grinding another diamond against it. This is called bruting and it forms the girdle or edge of the diamond.

Then the facets are ground on to the diamond. The diamond is held in a clamp whose angles can be adjusted. The clamp is held in a metal arm the back of which rests on two legs while the end holding the diamond is placed on the scaife, a large cast iron disc which spins like a potter's wheel. The scaife is specially dressed with fine grooves and charged with oil and diamond powder.

This is done by hand with frequent removal for inspection of progress. First, the 16 main facets, 8 on the crown and 8 on the pavilion, as well as the table and culet are put on by the blocker, who at this time determines the proportions and angles of the stone, a major economic decision. Finally, the brillianteerer grinds the remaining 40 facets.

Diamond has different hardnesses in different planes through the crystal, and each facet has it's own "grain" and must be set on the wheel with a different orientation. Diamond cannot be polished along its hardest direction, parallel to the triangular faces of the octahedron (double pyramid).

Unlike other gemstones, the cutting of which requires the facets to be ground several times with progressively finer abrasives to achieve a final polish, diamonds are cut and polished on the wheel simultaneously. It is not precisely understood how this occurs, but it is thought that carbon atoms are scraped off the diamond by being converted to graphite. There are no microscopic diamond chips in the polishing residue and the diamond surface is smooth down to the nanometer level.

In cutting round diamonds, 40% to 60% of the rough is ground away, so you can see the temptation of retaining more weight at the expense of proper proportions.

Though the octahedral shape of diamond rough is common, much rough looks like irregular pebbles owing to dissolution after formation, perhaps on the explosive trip to the surface. The shape of the rough determines the shape of the gem that will be cut from it.

Flattened, thin rough, called macles, are the result of a process called twinning, in which the crystal growth changes orientation in the middle of formation. Macles are cut into pear, marquise, or triangle shapes. Irregular rough is cut into whatever shape will yield the most valuable diamond or combination of diamonds.

Computer measuring and imaging systems are used to determine the most valuable yield from a piece of rough diamond. Some diamonds are cut entirely by automatic machines.

The Four C's: Carat weight, Color, Clarity, Cut.

3. Carats — Weight and Size

A carat is a unit of weight, not size[2]. A 6.5mm diamond weighs about 1 carat, while an identical cubic zirconia weighs 1.65 carat because cubic zirconia is 1.65 times more dense than diamond.

A carat is defined as 2/10ths of a gram. A dollar bill weighs 1 gram, or 5 carats(!). Diamonds are weighed to 1/100th of a carat, which is called a point. Thus a 50 pointer is .50, or ½ carat.

Nominal sizes for round diamonds   *Fig. 4*

Carats	1/4	1/2	3/4	1	1 1/2	2
Size	4.1mm	5.2mm	5.8mm	6.5mm	7.4mm	8.2mm

Variations in proportions will yield diamonds of the same carat weight that have different sizes. Well-cut diamonds tend to be smaller in size than diamonds that have been "spread" to give the consumer the illusion of more size for the money. This is especially true of the pear and marquise, which are often cut very thin (and lifeless). Another trick is to add weight by thickening the girdle or making the diamond too steep on the top or bottom, usually to the detriment of brilliance, to give the consumer the illusion of more carat for the money. Such diamonds are smaller in size than well-cut diamonds of the same weight.

Different shapes that weigh the same will appear to be different sizes due to the nature of the cut. Trillions have a larger size for the weight, princess cuts and emerald cuts may have a smaller apparent size for the weight.

Nominal Sizes for 1 Carat Diamonds of Different Shapes   *Fig. 5*

---

2. The carat, the unit of weight for gems is derived from the carob bean. The carob, or locust tree, grows in the Middle East. In ancient times, merchants found that dried carob beans were very uniform in weight.

Common Diamond Shapes

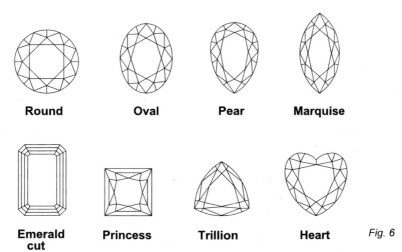

| Round | Oval | Pear | Marquise |

| Emerald cut | Princess | Trillion | Heart | *Fig. 6* |

In jewelry with many small diamonds or with diamond stud ear-rings, the total weight of all the diamonds together is usually given and abbreviated "t.w.", i.e. .47 ct. t.w. But I sometimes see this done inappropriately with a piece of jewelry with a center stone of significant size, say over 1/3 carat, and a number of accent stones. In such a case, the weight of the center and the total weight of the smaller diamonds should be given separately.

Total weights are supposed to be accurate to within ½ point (.005 carat), but this is often not the case, especially in mass-produced jewelry. A parcel of 100 3 pointers will actually weigh from say, 2.80 to 3.20 carats. But busy diamond setters can't be bothered to shuttle back and forth to the scale to weigh the diamonds for each piece. Or one of the diamonds will be a little too big for the setting and he'll grab a smaller one, altering the total weight. Baguettes are notorious for not fitting in the setting, requiring much trial and error.

So the manufacturer will simply give a nominal total weight, i.e. .30 carat for a piece with 10 stones from that 3 point parcel, or an average total weight, i.e. .29 carat each for 10 pieces made from a 2.90 carat parcel of 100 stones. If a number of jewelry pieces all have even total weights, i.e. .25 ct., 1.00 ct., etc., these are probably nominal, not actual weights. This is a sin, but usually a small one. However, occasionally the Jewelers Vigilance Committee, an industry watchdog, rips apart mass-produced pieces and finds serious discrepancies.

4. Color — White to the Eye and White to the Mind's Eye

Diamonds do occur in all colors (the Hope diamond in the Smithsonian is dark blue). But here we are concerned with colorless diamonds.

The universally used color-grading system is that of the GIA (Gemological Institute of America). This system uses letters from D to Z to describe increasing yellow or brown tints, usually caused by nitrogen impurities in diamonds.

GIA Color Scale

D – F	Colorless
G – J	Near Colorless
K – M	Faint Yellow
N – R	Very Light Yellow
S – Z	Light Yellow

The top three grades, D, E, and F can't be distinguished in diamonds of less than ¼ carat. A diamond rating a D color is completely colorless, completely transparent, and very rare. Diamonds rating D, E, and F are all colorless and are distinguished by slight differences in transparency rather than color. Color concentrates slightly at the facet edges. Diamond wholesalers pass out a white card-stock folding tray for color grading (with their company name on it). When a diamond is put in the tray and the sides of the tray are pinched to narrow the opening, color is more easily seen. If the pavilion facet edges look washed out and are more difficult to see when the diamond is put in this tray, the diamond is D-F in color. This is subtle and requires experience to spot.

G, H. and some I diamonds look colorless when mounted. You will probably not notice color in a mounted diamond over ¾ carat until the color reaches I or J, depending on the size of the diamond. Then you will see a faint darkening by comparison with a higher color stone once it is pointed out to you. At K, you will definitely see a yellow tint. Beyond Z, diamonds are considered to be colored, not "capes" as off-white diamonds are called.

Color is graded by comparison with a diamond or cubic zirconia master set in a white box under special low-ultraviolet fluorescent light. Diamond master sets are graded by the GIA against their master set. Most retailers use a cubic zirconia master set, since diamond master sets are very expensive. The GIA will not grade cubic zirconia so all cz master sets have been graded against diamonds at one remove from the standard or by a machine called a colorimeter.

A colorimeter prints out a little strip of paper giving the color grade of a diamond. I have a cubic zirconia master set that was calibrated by colorimeter. The lure of such a device is scientific objectivity, but these machines are also expensive. The GIA calls the colorimeter a useful tool but maintains that that grading by a trained human eye is still the final arbiter of color.

Exact color grades are not given for mounted diamonds, i.e. in appraisals, since the surrounding metal, especially yellow gold, and inability to position the diamond correctly, makes it impossible to distinguish the very faint differences in color between grades. A two or three grade range is given.

Sometimes diamonds "face-up" whiter than their grade, since color is graded from the bottom of a diamond to determine its true body color without the interference of the diamond's sparkle.

Don't get crazy about color in buying a diamond in the higher color grades. You will pay a lot more for an E or F versus a G, H, or I. Once the stone is mounted, you may not be able to see the difference, or, if you can, it may strike you as minor. Remember, G, H, I and J are all classified as near-colorless. These faint differences in color may be less apparent to the eye than to the mind's eye.

Since consumers have preconceived notions of what color is white enough, there are large price jumps between what consumers think of as white and not so white, H and I, in the more desirable clarity grades. But this is just the mind's eye looking at the alphabet.

I once sold a 2.44 carat diamond, a large stone in which color should be easy to see. The customer, in his mind's eye, wanted at least a G color. But the G color was more than his budget. I obtained both a G and an I color diamond for him to see. I put both diamonds in tweezers and asked him to go by the window and tell which was which. He was able to do it, but just barely. He realized that the difference in color was more in the mind's eye than the eye and he bought the I color.

Color is the most difficult property of a diamond to grade and, I suspect, the most abused.

You may have heard the term "blue-white" to portray the ultimate colorless diamond, like the whiter-than-white of a bleach commercial. Many diamonds light up blue under ultraviolet light ("black light"). This is called fluorescence. There is an ultraviolet component in daylight (4%) and artificial light, and lower color diamonds that also have strong blue fluorescence are thought to have a slightly improved, whiter color. Diamond firms in the 1930's sought out these diamonds and promoted them as "blue-white".

The advertising must have worked. Sixty years later people still talk of "blue-white" diamonds, although the meaning has been transformed from an off-white diamond that looks better than it should to a diamond to die for. The Federal Trade Commission prohibited this term in 1938. You are hereby officially forbidden to use the term "blue-white".

There are very strongly fluorescent stones, called Premiers (after the Premier mine in South Africa), that get a milky or hazy appearance in sunlight. This is definitely a defect. These stones are rare. I've only seen a few, although I've seen a number that appear hazy under the microscope's halogen light, but not in sunlight or indoor light. Occasionally, I get a sixth sense feeling that a diamond is strongly fluorescent and when I put it under the ultraviolet light, it is. I know I'm responding to some faint visual clue, but I haven't been able to put my finger on it. But I can't say that the appearance of these diamonds is adversely affected.

Wholesale price lists indicate a discount for strongly fluorescent stones in high color grades and a premium for low color fluorescent stones. This assumes that fluorescence will degrade the appearance of a high color stone and improve the appearance of a low color one, as in the blue-white business.

The GIA did a study of fluorescence in which 24 diamonds of different colors and degrees of fluorescence were viewed by 46 observers from both the jewelry trade and the general public. The study found that the non-trade observers saw no difference in color between the fluorescent and non-fluorescent diamonds, while the observers from the trade saw a better face-up color for the fluorescent stones. So don't get crazy about fluorescence, either.

Top light browns, or TLB's, are small diamonds used in cheap jewelry. I often see them set in 10 karat gold. The color is very noticeable, and not very attractive. Australia produces lots of brown diamonds, and they have to go somewhere.

Australian brown diamond production also gave birth to "Champagne" and "Cognac" diamonds. Brown diamonds are attractive if they're brown enough. But I've had a number of customers come in with "champagne" diamonds that were merely off-color. Champagne diamonds are the only colored diamonds that are affordable: they cost less than white diamonds.

5. Clarity — Through the Looking Glass

The clarity of a diamond refers to flaws or imperfections, which are called inclusions. A diamond is graded for clarity by judging the visibility of inclusions under 10X magnification. The most common inclusions are feathers and crystal inclusions. Feathers are breaks or cracks inside the stone that were caused by stresses during formation. Crystal inclusions are crystals of other minerals or diamond itself that were incorporated into the diamond as it grew. What some people call "carbon-spots" are actually included crystals that are dark or appear dark under certain lighting conditions. Or they may be coated with graphite due to reversion of diamond to graphite at the interface between the inclusion and the host diamond. The term "piqué" (pee-kay) is used for these inclusions.

Except for very large eye-visible feathers in the lowest clarity grades, feathers do not affect the durability of the diamond. After all, the diamond was subjected to far greater stress during cutting than you will be able to inflict upon it.

Very tiny crystals are called pinpoints and groups of pinpoints too small to be seen individually are called clouds. Graining, which looks like creases in cellophane, is caused by atomic irregularities in the diamond crystal.

Blemishes, which are surface rather then internal flaws, are taken into account under clarity. These include tiny nicks, pits, scratches, and polishing marks.

Naturals are small areas of the original crystal surface of the rough diamond that were not cut away during polishing to maximize the diameter of the stone. They are usually on or just underneath the girdle and they look like shiny irregular facets with sets of parallel striations, or, sometimes, perfect little triangles called trigons. Diamonds are often cut with naturals in pairs, on opposite sides of the diamond. This way the cutter maximizes the spread of the rough.

Small naturals that that are confined to the girdle and do not intrude into the stone or flatten its outline will not lower the clarity grade of a diamond except in the very highest grades. Naturals are unique to each diamond and serve as excellent identification characteristics

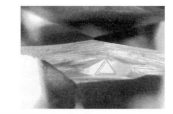

Fig. 7

The diamond in the left photograph is a rectangular princess cut. The large natural is on the bottom end facet, just below the girdle. The natural is actually recessed, like a flat-bottomed crater, perhaps a few hundredths of a millimeter deep. The ragged edge is its border. This natural has a spectacular forest of trigons.

The top right photo shows a large natural on and extending below the girdle of a round diamond. It sports a single trigon.

Trigons occur on the triangular faces of the double pyramids of rough diamonds, with the point of the trigon facing the base of the pyramid. Naturals are fairly common on diamonds, but naturals with trigons are not. Naturals that actually penetrate the stone, as in the bottom photograph, are called indented naturals. (The light-colored triangle in the photo is the bottom of the indented natural, which is fairly deep.)

The following are the eleven GIA clarity grades.

Flawless — no inclusions or blemishes. Nothing to be seen at 10X magnification.

Internally Flawless — no inclusions, minor blemishes.

Very Very Slightly Included (VVS1 and VVS2) — minute inclusions, very difficult to see. The VVS grades are extremely stringent, just a few tiny pinpoints or minute feathers.

Very slightly Included (VS1 and VS2) — minor inclusions. You'll see them clearly under the microscope once they're pointed out to you, but they'll strike you as very minor.

Slightly included (SI1 and SI2) — easily seen inclusions not visible face-up to the naked eye, sometimes visible through the pavilion. Most people would frown at an SI2 seen under the microscope.

Imperfect (I1, I2, I3) — Inclusions obvious under magnification and may be eye-visible. In the lower grades the transparency of the stone is degraded and durability may be in question.

The major wholesale price sheet (see page 75) uses an SI3 grade, reflecting a need to discriminate among the better I1's, since many lower clarity diamonds are being sold these days, and an I1 grade can be the kiss of death for a diamond. The GIA has not adopted the SI3 grade, nor has the trade in general.

The following through-the-microscope photographs illustrate common inclusions in diamonds and should give you some sense of clarity grading. Due to the limitations of digital photography and printing, they are not as detailed as you would see with your eyes. Also, the microscope lighting may make some light inclusions, especially feathers, appear dark. This is the only way they would show up on the photograph.

Fig. 8

There are two very small crystal inclusions indicated by the circles in this .71 carat diamond, which the GIA graded VS1

Fig. 9

This D color .77 carat marquise was graded VS2 by the GIA. The feather is only dark under microscope lighting and is completely invisible to the eye.

These three inclusions are actually light in color. The one on the right is a nest of small cracks. Due to their number and central location, this diamond grades SI1.

Fig. 10

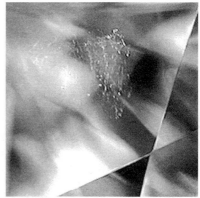

The network of small cracks just under the surface of the table in this 2.45 carat diamond, although somewhat large, is barely visible, even under the microscope. I graded this diamond SI1. If this inclusion were more prominent in appearance the diamond would be SI2.

Fig. 11

These bright inclusions under the table of this .33 carat grade SI1

Fig. 12

This feather and other inclusions make this diamond an SI2.

Fig. 13

The white color and size of this feather is a tough call. This diamond earring is borderline between SI2 and I1.

Fig. 14

This diamond has numerous prominent inclusions which also are reflected around the stone. It grades I1. The circled inclusions at the bottom are needle-like crystals.

Fig. 15

This large centrally located white feather grades I2.

Fig. 16

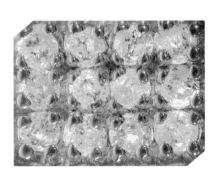

Fig. 17

The small diamonds in this 10 karat gold man's ring are full of cracks and black crystals. They grade I2-I3. They have no brilliance.

Clarity grading is subjective, with the GIA definitions of the grades as guidelines. There are borderline cases that could go either way.

I once did an appraisal on a diamond that had a good-size SI1 feather looking at it from the bottom. But face-up, the feather appeared much smaller and on the edge of the diamond, a VS2 feather. Since it was an insurance appraisal and it would be unlikely that a similar diamond could be found to replace it, I graded it VS2. If it were replaced with a diamond with a much larger SI1 feather face-up, the client could well object that the appearance of the replacement is inferior, since diamonds are viewed from the top and not from the bottom.

In general, inclusions in the SI or better grades do not affect the appearance of a diamond since they are not visible to the eye, nor will they degrade its brilliance. Light scattering from these features is infinitesimal. I once saw a diamond that that had a network of small cracks throughout the stone. Yet, since it was well cut, it was very brilliant. Brilliance will only be affected by very large inclusions in the imperfect grades, especially large feathers located deep in the center that block light in the heart of the stone, or by extensive smaller inclusions that make the diamond look cloudy.

Large or numerous black inclusions that are reflected around inside the diamond will make it look grayish or blackish in color.

But even if an inclusion is not eye-visible, people generally want higher clarity grades for engagement ring diamonds. This is the mind's eye looking at the purity of the symbol of a couple's union, and it is perfectly understandable. An I1 or SI2 inclusion can look pretty gruesome blown up under the microscope.

For diamond earrings or everyday diamond jewelry, they are usually willing to accept lower clarity to keep the cost down.

It's up to you to sort out what is acceptable to the eye, the mind's eye, and the pocketbook.

6. Cut – How A Diamond Shines

Cut is what makes a diamond shine. The cut or "make" of a diamond refers not to the number of facets, but to their angles and relative sizes. A diamond is an analog light computer. The program is the angles and sizes of the facets. The output is brilliance.

When light enters a diamond it is bent inwards by the diamond, then bounces around inside until it comes out, where it is bent outwards. The idea behind designing a diamond is to control this bending and bouncing so that the light comes out the top of the diamond and at an angle that is directed towards the eye.

By putting the correct angles on the facets and making them the correct relative sizes, the maximum brilliance and fire, the spreading of light into colors like a prism, and the optimum balance between brilliance and fire, are achieved. There's very little tolerance for some of these dimensions, less than ± 1° on the bottom angle, which determines the fundamental brilliance of the diamond.

Due to the typical shapes of rough diamonds it is more wasteful, and thereby more expensive, to cut a diamond to ideal proportions. As was discussed before, the idea of an optically correct round diamond has been around since 1919. But most diamonds are deliberately cut more or less incorrectly because consumer values are out of balance, abetted by the jewelry trade.

Since cut concerns a number of factors, it can't be nailed down with one number and there is no cut grade[3] in the sense of a brilliance grade, which would in any case be highly subjective. There are only angles and percentages, which are meaningful to the gemologist but not to the consumer.

Clarity and color grades, however, are neat pigeonholes and consumers fasten on to these rather than trust their eyes. In the better grades you can't see any flaws with the eye and color differences are faint, so grading comes to the fore. Non-gemologist jewelers are often ignorant of cut also and reinforce this pigeonholing by selling diamonds solely on clarity and color.

People often go diamond shopping with color and clarity in mind, or brag about how white or clean their diamond is, but few demand

---

3. The American Gem Society (AGS) does have a cut grade that entails deductions from an ideal cut. This is discussed in detail on page 46. The AGS was founded as a sister organization to the GIA in 1934 by Robert M. Shipley, who had started the GIA in 1931. The AGS has strict ethical rules for its members, who are individuals, not stores. The AGS is a generally upscale jewelers organization. Only 1400 of the 40,000 jewelry stores in the U.S. Are AGS member firms, with AGS "Titleholders".

a fine cut. The irony is that brilliance and fire, though not formally graded, are the things you can see with your eye and should be the primary factor in buying a diamond. Don't get so carried away with the idea of the purity and whiteness of a diamond that you forget the whole reason for buying a diamond in the first place: to dazzle the eye.

A diamond is a precariously balanced optical system. Make the bottom just slightly too steep and the light coming out the top angles away from the eye and the diamond looks dark in the center. Too shallow and no light comes from the center and the diamond looks dead. Too large a table and fire diminishes and scintillation, sparkle as the diamond moves, becomes unbalanced.

The brilliance of a diamond that delights our eye may be considered as the simultaneous interaction of four different processes: refraction, dispersion, reflection, and scintillation.

Refraction

The crown and pavilion of a diamond function as a lens and reflector system for light. The crown steers light from a variety of directions onto the pavilion facets. The pavilion facets then reflect light back to the top of the diamond, where the crown facets guide it to the eye.

One of the properties of any transparent substance is that it bends light entering it from the air. This bending is called refraction. The displaced image of a spoon in a glass of water is an example of refraction.

Diamond bends light more than almost any other natural material and this is the key to its brilliance. The amount of bending of a ray of light as it enters the diamond varies with the angle it strikes a facet.

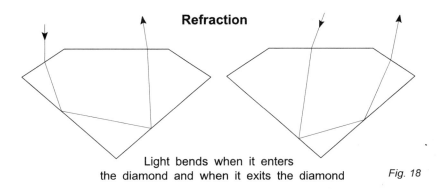

Refraction

Light bends when it enters
the diamond and when it exits the diamond

Fig. 18

Light hitting straight on to the facet is not bent at all. As the angle gets lower and lower, the light is forced to deviate more and more strongly away from its original path, bending inwards towards an imaginary line perpendicular to the facet. As the entering light ray runs parallel to a facet, it is deflected over 65° and a limit is reached as this is the last ray that can get into the diamond. This limit of maximum bending is called the critical angle. The critical angle of diamond is about 24.5°, measured from the vertical.

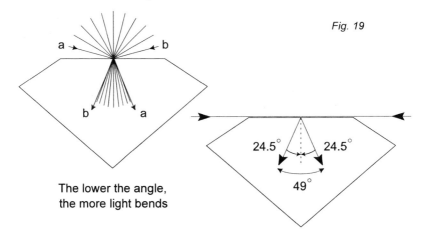

Fig. 19

The lower the angle,
the more light bends

Angle of maximum refraction = critical angle

No matter from what direction a light ray hits a crown facet it will be channeled toward the pavilion facets within a narrow range of directions which may be imagined as a cone of 49° (twice the critical angle, see diagram). The small critical angle[4] of diamond will concentrate light coming from all directions into 27% of them (49° out of the possible 180° of the straight line of a facet).

The job of the pavilion facets is to reflect light back out the top of a diamond so you can see it. Once inside the diamond, light behaves differently. Outside the diamond, light from any angle can enter it. At low angles, a lot of light is reflected, but some always goes in.

4.. Light zips through the air at 186,000 miles per second. When it enters a diamond it slows down to 77,000 miles per second. The ratio of the speed of light in air to the speed of light in a substance is called its refractive index. Diamond, at 2.417, has a higher refractive index than all but a few obscure gems. The higher the refractive index the smaller the critical angle and the more brilliant the gem. Other commonly seen transparent natural gems fall in the range 1.54 (quartz) to 1.98 (zircon). Standard refractometer instruments can measure the refractive index of a gemstone only up to 1.81.

Inside the diamond, light hitting a facet is either completely reflected back inside the diamond to hit another facet, or it exits completely into the air. It's all or nothing. This phenomenon occurs in any transparent material and has to do with crossing the boundary between the tightly packed atoms of the material and the much less dense atoms of the air.

Whether the pavilion facets completely reflect the light back towards the top of the diamond, as is desirable, or the light passes through to leak out the bottom depends on the angle the light hits these facets. Light that strikes these facets outside the critical angle cone is reflected; light that hits inside the critical angle cone passes out the bottom of the stone.

Inside the diamond the critical angle defines a 27% escape window. By comparison, typical glass has a critical angle cone of about 84° which gives a window of almost 47%. This is why a glass, or "paste" stone (or a low brilliance stone, such as aquamarine) looks watery.

Light Loss From Incorrect Pavilion Angle

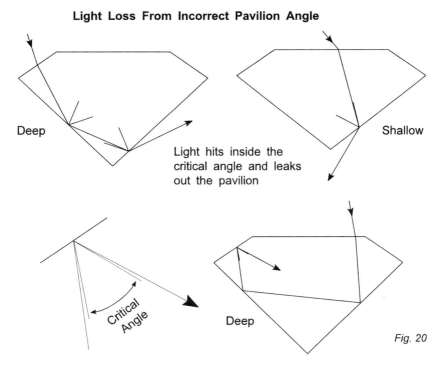

Fig. 20

Light hits outside the critical angle and is reflected back into the diamond

28

Since the crown facets funnel light into a narrow cone, the pavilion facets must be oriented so as to intercept the light outside the critical angle escape window so it will be reflected. A well-cut (and clean) diamond looks almost silvery, like a mirror, under bright overhead lights. This is visual evidence of the total reflection of light.

Actually, the pavilion facets must prevent the escape of light twice. Since light has to make a U-turn to be reflected back out the top, it must bounce from one pavilion facet across the diamond to another pavilion facet, then up and out the top of the diamond. Any error in the angle of the pavilion facets is doubled, since light must reflect from them twice. So it is of supreme importance that the bottom of the diamond be cut with the correct slope. The crown angles are less sensitive. Few light rays entering through the crown also exit through the crown. Most light that enters through a crown facet exits through the table or vice-versa, encountering the crown once.

Sometimes this total internal reflection can have untoward consequences. Inclusions situated on one side of the diamond can appear as perfect mirror images on the other side of the diamond. A centrally located inclusion deep inside the diamond can be reflected by each pavilion facet, forming a ring of reflected images, degrading the clarity of the stone. These are called reflecting inclusions. So perfect a mirror is a diamond that it can be very difficult for diamond cutters to determine which is the inclusion and which is the reflection. This is important when attempting to divide a rough diamond so as to eliminate the inclusion or place it favorably.

Crown and pavilion angles are measured from the horizontal and are for the 8 crown main facets and the 8 pavilion main facets.

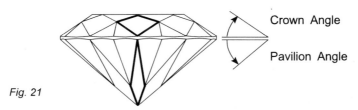

Crown Angle

Pavilion Angle

Fig. 21

The diagrams on the next page illustrate the effects on brilliance of the pavilion angle. These diagrams are the result of a computer program I wrote and are highly simplified – two dimensional and just for the main facets and just for overhead light – but accord with the visual appearance of diamonds with too shallow or too deep pavilions: deep diamonds are dark in the center and shallow diamonds are dead in the center.

Very shallow diamonds show a reflection of the girdle just inside the table as a whitish ring. Such a diamond is called a fish-eye. Very deep diamonds look so dark in the center they're called nailheads. (see photos next page).

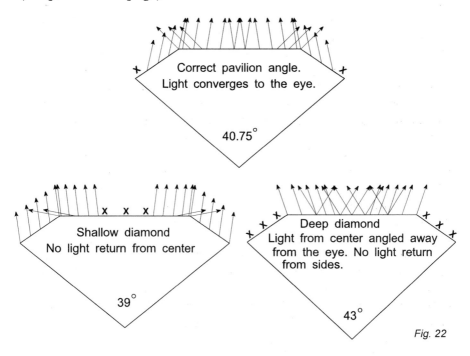

Light Return From Main Facets - Overhead Light

The size of the reflection of the table in the pavilion can be used to estimate the all-important pavilion angle. The steeper the pavilion angle, the higher up in the pavilion is the table reflection. This makes it appear larger and darker. The shallower the pavilion angle, the smaller and lighter the reflection. The photos on the next 3 pages show this clearly. This reflection is visible to the naked eye in larger diamonds and stands out in ad photos and TV close-ups.

These photos are provided to help you spot the dogs and recognize the good ones when they are clear. But judging pavilion angles by these reflections can be tricky when they are indistinct, which is often the case with shallow diamonds. Don't get a-little-bit-of knowledge overconfident. It takes experience to always know the meaning of what you see.

This small single-cut diamond is a very bad fish-eye. The stone is so shallow that the gray area occupying most of the center is a reflection of the entire girdle, which is thick and coarse. The black area on the lower right is an inclusion. *Fig. 23*

The table reflection is actually so small it breaks up and can be misleading. But the white ring inside the table is a reflection of the girdle and pegs this stone as a fish-eye, a shallow diamond. *Fig. 24*

This is a classic nailhead. The dark table reflection fills the center of the stone and is obvious to the unaided eye. This diamond has little shine.

Fig. 25

The table reflection in this stone is far too large and indicates a very deep pavilion. The diamond has poor brilliance.

Fig. 26

Fig. 27

The table reflection occupies over half the area of the table in these two diamonds. While an improvement over the preceding examples, These diamonds are too deep for good brilliance. The white area at 7:00 on the right photo is a chip. A side view of this diamond is on page 39.

The table reflection takes up just over half the area of the table. This .64 carat diamond was slightly dark in the center and noticeably less brilliant when compared with a diamond with an ideal pavilion angle.

Fig. 28

This diamond has a pavilion angle within the ideal range. The small black triangles around the table reflection are reflections of the star facets and normally appear dark like this.

Fig. 29

Fig. 30

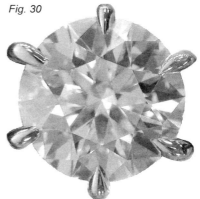

These two diamonds also have pavilion angles close to ideal. The .26 carat diamond on the right has a rare 53% table.

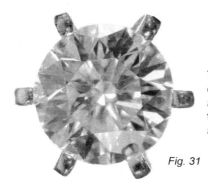

The table reflection of this ideal cut diamond indicates a correct pavilion angle. Its octagonal shape is due to the perfect symmetry of this "hearts and arrows" diamond. (See page 49).

Fig. 31

The crown angle and table size can also be estimated visually.

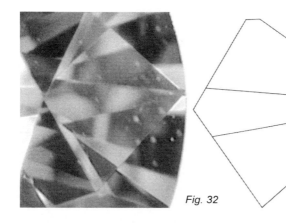

This reflection of the opposite pavilion main facet in the crown main indicates a crown angle in the normal range

Fig. 32

Fig. 33

This is a reflection of the pavilion main facet on the opposite side of the diamond in a crown main facet, and indicates a very steep crown. The entire facet down to the culet is visible. The diamond must be level and this reflection appear in all 8 crown main facets, since a tilted diamond will look like this on the high side. Diamonds that show these reflections have a characteristic lace-edge look under the microscope.

We met this nasty little fellow before, in the clarity section. The crown on this diamond is exceptionally steep, with reflections of the large culet visible in the crown mains. This diamond has the lace-edge look.

Fig. 34

34

Fig. 35

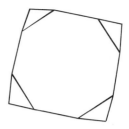

The outline of the table and star facets bows out for this large 65% table.

Fig. 36

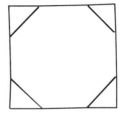

With this 60% table the table and star facet outline is straight. The outline is skewed a bit because the symmetry is off.

Fig. 37

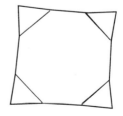

The table and star facet outline bows in for this 55.8% table. The bowing is somewhat exaggerated because the stars are slightly long.

Dispersion

When light is bent as it enters the diamond, the different colors that make up white light are bent by slightly different amounts and begin to spread as by a prism.[5] Once started, they continue to diverge as they travel through the diamond. The bigger the diamond, the longer the light path and the more the colors separate.

When light exits the top of the diamond, it is bent again, though in the opposite direction, since it is crossing a boundary between the diamond and the air rather than vice-versa, and this separates the colors even more.

Remember the business about refraction? The lower the angle (as long as it's within the critical angle escape window so the light won't be reflected back into the diamond), the more the bending. If the crown facets are oriented such that light reflected from the pavilion hits them at lower angles, just inside the critical angle, they'll give a nice final push to this color-spreading.

The visual result of this prism effect is called dispersion, or fire, and any diamond you buy should have lots of it. However, size matters. You won't see as much fire in a smaller diamonds because the spreading of the colors develops less due to the shorter length of the light path.

So the correct crown angle is is important for dispersion. Too shallow and the exiting light hits at a higher angle and is not bent as much, both on the way in and the way out of the diamond, and the colors don't separate as much. Too steep a crown and light will either be reflected back into the diamond or be angled away from the eye.

The size of the table as well as the crown angle also affects dispersion. A large table reduces the size of the other crown facets. This reduces fire by reducing the area on which it occurs.

---

5. Actually, a transparent material has a different refractive index for each wavelength, or color, of light. The longer wavelengths of red light are bent more and the shorter wavelengths of blue light are bent less. Published refractive indices for gemstones are measured using a standard yellow light. Dispersion is measured as the difference in refractive index of certain wavelengths at the extremes of the visible light spectrum, in the violet and in the red. The dispersion of diamond is thus determined to be .044, which is exceeded by only a few natural gems (notably, demantoid, a rare green garnet, at .057). So the potential for fire is inherent in the material itself. It only needs to be realized by proper cutting.

Reflection

Much more light striking a diamond will be reflected and never get into it than with other gems. 17% of light striking a diamond perpendicular to a facet will be reflected rather than enter the stone. Even more light will be reflected at lower angles (you can see this effect by looking at your watch straight on and then tilting it about 70° away from you – you'll see a reflection of ceiling lights in the watch crystal).

This inherent reflectance of diamond is almost four times greater than quartz (i.e. Amethyst). This is why diamond has its characteristic "adamantine" luster and other gems look glassy.

This high reflectance, along with perfectly flat, sharp-edged facets and high polish due to diamond's incredible hardness, produces flashes of reflected light that is part of the impression of brilliance we see in a diamond. Reflectance is influenced by the quality of the polish and also by the size of the table. A large table gives too powerful a flash compared to the other crown facets and gives an unbalanced appearance.

Scintillation

As the diamond, the light source, or your head moves, sparkle, or twinkle, is seen. This is called scintillation. Movement causes reflections from the pavilion facets to be broken up as they sweep across different facets on the crown and they come at the eye from a variety of different directions and angles. Scintillation is dependent on proper crown and pavilion angles, since scintillation is brilliance in motion, as well as the size of the table. Marquises and pears have the most scintillation, especially around the points of the stones. Emerald cuts have the least scintillation.

The Girdle

The girdle, or edge, of the diamond is an important element of the cut. Girdles are graded *extremely thin, very thin, thin, medium, slightly thick, very thick, extremely thick*. Commonly there is a variance in the girdle in which case a range is given, describing the thinnest and thickest parts, i.e, thin-medium.

An extremely thin girdle is a knife-edge girdle and this can be a problem. Knife-edge girdles set in prongs in a ring such that the girdle is exposed invariably chip[6], sometimes seriously. A chip can take a bite out of the edge of the stone or run down the pavilion or crown, taking out a slice. A chipped diamond would have to be recut, reducing the diameter of the stone by the depth of the chip plus a little to build up a new girdle. This means a loss of weight and value as well. And there is cost and risk in having a diamond recut. Watch out for knife-edge girdles. I once saw a diamond that had small chips completely around the stone due to a knife-edge girdle. Luckily, there were no large chips. Or cut fingers – the diamond was like a serrated steak knife.

I've also seen diamonds that were chipped in the process of setting, when a prong was being pulled down. This was unbeknownst to the customer, being discovered years later in the course of a routine pre-repair microscope examination. When resetting customers' diamonds, I warn them that there's a risk with knife-edge girdles, and I'm usually unwilling to attempt to set such a diamond in a bezel, which requires hammering the metal of the setting over the stone.

Thick girdles give useless extra weight to a diamond, yielding a stone that is small for its weight. The most extreme example I have seen was a 1 carat round diamond whose diameter was that of a ¾ carat. The girdle was extremely thick and the crown was also steep, adding extra weight on the top as well. The price the customer paid was great for a 1 carat, but just about right for a ¾ carat. In other words, the customer got exactly what he paid for.

Diamonds with thick girdles are also difficult to set properly, leaving gaps between the edge of the diamond and the notch of the prongs that will become packed with dirt.

Wavy girdles unbalance the arrangement of of the adjacent facets and indicate trouble if severe. Girdles that vary too much in thickness, encompassing two or more grades, i.e., thin-thick, can indicate problems also. Although if the cutter was chasing an inclusion by making one pavilion facet a little steeper and thinning the girdle in just one spot, it's not a big deal as long as the girdle isn't a knife-edge in that place.

---

6. It is commonly believed that a diamond can't be chipped. Diamond is the hardest gem, but hardness, resistance to scratching, is not the same as toughness, resistance to cracking or chipping. Nephrite, one of the two unrelated minerals called jade, is the toughest — you can scratch it, but you could use a block of it as an anvil without chipping it. The reason why is that unlike diamond, which is a single crystal, nephrite jade is a mass of microscopic, fibrous, interlocking crystals.

A *bruted* girdle is one that is ground but not polished. Rough, coarsely ground girdles look sugary and will trap dirt that is very difficult to get out. This can darken the entire stone as it is reflected around inside the diamond. Fancy shapes usually have a faceted girdle and may have more variance in girdle thickness than rounds, especially at the points of pears and marquises and in the clefts of hearts. Occasionally, I see a girdle that is polished, but not faceted, but these are uncommon.

Fig. 38

This diamond chipped badly due to its extremely thin girdle.

This 6mm diamond weighs .92 ct. It should weigh about .80 ct. The very thick girdle and a very steep crown of 38.9° pumps it up to the next weight and price category.

Fig. 39

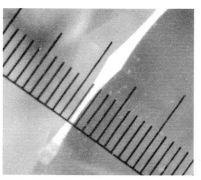

This very thin girdle is less than .1mm thick, thinner than a sheet of paper, in one spot. The thin spot was carefully placed under a prong.

Fig. 40

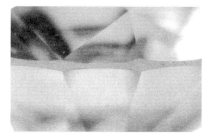

This is a classic medium bruted girdle.

Fig. 41

Symmetry and Polish

Symmetry refers to the facets lining up with each other, being symmetrically shaped and all meeting at a point. Polish features include fine polish lines and white drag marks from the polishing wheel, scratches, small nicks, etc.

Symmetry and polish are graded *poor, fair, good, very good,* and *excellent.* Very good or excellent grades are the highest expression of the cutters art and are difficult to achieve.

Polish would have to be pretty bad to affect the beauty of a diamond. Don't be concerned unless the polish is graded poor.

There is little effect on the appearance of the diamond in good or better symmetry grades. Fair or poor means something major is wrong, such as an off-center table or culet, or noticeable crown/pavilion misalignment, the crown twisted relative to the pavilion such that the crown and pavilion main facets don't line up with each other. This could affect brilliance.

Symmetry has become the final frontier for diamonds. Branded ideal cuts, in order to differentiate themselves from generic diamonds of identical angles and proportions are touting perfection in symmetry – even beyond a GIA grade of excellent – as a selling point and to justify their premium prices. There'll be more on this in chapter 8 on ideal cuts.

7. Certificates — Have Your Papers in Order

There are a number of gemological laboratories, including foreign ones, that offer quality reports for diamonds, in which diamonds are graded. They are obtained by the wholesaler or retailer. These reports are called certificates by the trade.

The GIA's Gem Trade Laboratory is the top of the pecking order. The GIA will only grade loose stones. A GIA certificate does not give a dollar value for a diamond. It's not an appraisal[7], it's a grading document.

It gives the carat weight and measurements, including the table and total depth, both in millimeters and as a percentage of the diameter. It also grades girdle thickness, culet size, polish and symmetry, and reports fluorescence. Inclusions and blemishes are plotted on a diagram of the diamond. (See p.91 for an example of a plot).

There is no cut grade. Polish and symmetry grades are not a cut grade. As of now (Aug. 2002), the GIA has said it will include more cut information on its certificates in the future, but that it hasn't yet decided what that will be. Pavilion and crown angles would be a welcome addition. They are fundamental to assessing diamond cut and could easily be obtained by machine.

Recently, the GIA introduced a mini-certificate, called a Diamond Dossier, for smaller diamonds. The Diamond Dossier has everything except the clarity plot, which is time-consuming since it is done by hand. Diamond Dossiers are available for diamonds as small as ¼ carat.

In 1996, the American Gem Society opened a grading laboratory and began issuing certificates. The AGS certificate does give a cut grade (see footnote on page 25). This will be explained in the next chapter on ideal cuts.

A certificate is especially useful in nailing down the color grade, which is the most subjective and difficult property to grade and the one most likely to be misrepresented. It is also good for settling borderline clarity grades.

---

7. Some certificates do give a dollar value for the diamonds they grade. One certificate I saw gave a price that was ridiculously inflated, 6 times the wholesale price. Standard appraisal methodology requires that the appraisal price be the most commonly occurring price in the typical store in which it is sold in the area the customer lives. Certificates are usually obtained by the wholesaler and the laboratory can have no advance idea of the type or location of the store in which it will be sold. And in any case, no one sells diamonds at a 6 time markup. See the chapter on appraisals, p. 85.

There's a certain politics to certificates. If a diamond was submitted to a laboratory other than the GIA for grading, there's probably a reason for it. One wholesaler told me that he sends diamonds he feels have borderline color grades to another lab because there's a better chance of getting the higher grade. A diamond is usually sent to the AGS for grading because it will get a cut grade. An AGS ideal cut grade will carry a premium price. Diamonds with certificates other than GIA or AGS are discounted. In practice, a diamond isn't a D color or flawless unless the GIA says it is.

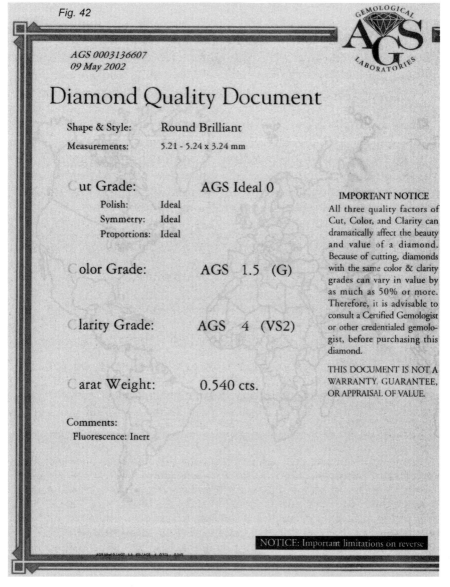

Fig. 42

AGS 0003136607
09 May 2002

Diamond Quality Document

Shape & Style: Round Brilliant

Measurements: 5.21 - 5.24 x 3.24 mm

Cut Grade: AGS Ideal 0

Polish: Ideal
Symmetry: Ideal
Proportions: Ideal

Color Grade: AGS 1.5 (G)

Clarity Grade: AGS 4 (VS2)

Carat Weight: 0.540 cts.

Comments:
Fluorescence: Inert

IMPORTANT NOTICE
All three quality factors of Cut, Color, and Clarity can dramatically affect the beauty and value of a diamond. Because of cutting, diamonds with the same color & clarity grades can vary in value by as much as 50% or more. Therefore, it is advisable to consult a Certified Gemologist or other credentialed gemologist, before purchasing this diamond.

THIS DOCUMENT IS NOT A WARRANTY, GUARANTEE, OR APPRAISAL OF VALUE.

NOTICE: Important limitations on reverse

The AGS and GIA certificates reproduced here have been modified by rearranging components and removing white space to fit them on the page.

Key to Symbols

Bruise	✕	Crystal	○	Laser Drill Hole	◉
Cavity	⊘	Extra Facet	∧	Natural	∧
Chip	∧	Feather	⌒	Needle	╱
Cleavage	⫽	Indented Natural	⩘	Pinpoint	•
Cloud	∴	Knot	◎	Twinning Wisp	⤳

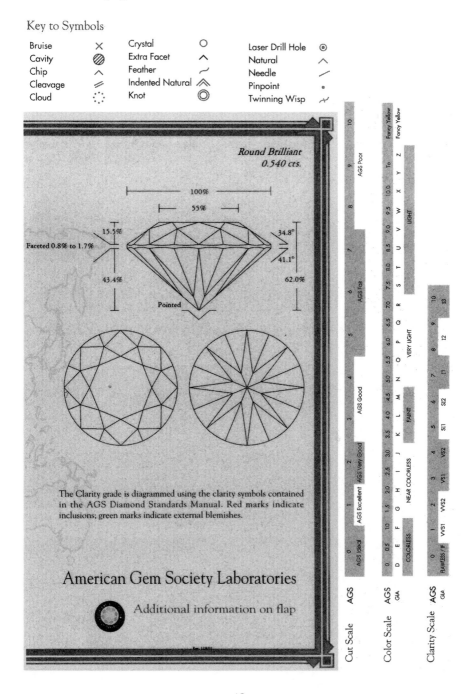

Round Brilliant
0.540 cts.

100%
55%
15.5%
Faceted 0.8% to 1.7%
34.8°
41.1°
43.4%
62.0%
Pointed

The Clarity grade is diagrammed using the clarity symbols contained in the AGS Diamond Standards Manual. Red marks indicate inclusions; green marks indicate external blemishes.

American Gem Society Laboratories

Additional information on flap

Fig. 43

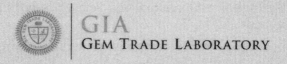

GIA
GEM TRADE LABORATORY

DIAMOND GRADING REPORT

May 01, 2001

Shape and Cutting Style .... ROUND BRILLIANT
   Measurements ....5.75 - 5.78 x 3.55 mm
   Weight .... 0.71 carat

Proportions
   Depth .... 61.6 %
   Table .... 60 %
   Girdle .... THIN TO MEDIUM
   Culet .... VERY SMALL

Finish
   Polish .... VERY GOOD
   Symmetry .... VERY GOOD

Clarity Grade VS1

Color Grade .... H

Fluorescence .... NONE

Comments:
Internal graining is not shown.

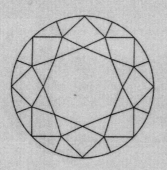

KEY TO SYMBOLS
  ° Crystal

GIA REPORT 11526765

New York Headquarters
580 Fifth Avenue | New York, NY 10036-4794
T: 212-221-5858 | F: 212-575-3095

Carlsbad
5355 Armada Drive | Carlsbad, CA 92008-4699
T: 760-603-4500 | F: 760-603-1814

78713201

GIA CLARITY SCALE

- FLAWLESS
- INTERNALLY FLAWLESS
- VVS$_1$ | VERY VERY SLIGHTLY INCLUDED
- VVS$_2$
- VS$_1$ | VERY SLIGHTLY INCLUDED
- VS$_2$
- SI$_1$ | SLIGHTLY INCLUDED
- SI$_2$
- I$_1$ | INCLUDED
- I$_2$
- I$_3$

GIA COLOR SCALE

- D | COLORLESS
- E
- F
- G | NEAR COLORLESS
- H
- I
- J
- K | FAINT
- L
- M
- N
- O | VERY LIGHT
- P
- Q
- R
- S
- T
- U | LIGHT
- V
- W
- X
- Y
- Z

This Report is not a guarantee, valuation or appraisal. This Report contains only the characteristics of the diamond described herein after it has been graded, tested, examined and analyzed by GIA Gem Trade Laboratory under 10X magnification, and/or has been inscribed, using the techniques and equipment available to GIA Gem Trade Laboratory at the time of the examination and/or at the time of being inscribed, including fully corrected triplet loupe and binocular microscope, master color comparison diamonds, standardized viewing environment and light source, electronic carat balance, synthetic diamond screening device, high intensity short wave fluorescence imaging system, short wave ultraviolet transmission detection system, optical measuring device, micro laser inscribing device, ProportionScope®, ultraviolet lamps, millimeter gauge, and ancillary instruments as necessary. Red symbols denote internal characteristics (inclusions). Green or black symbols denote external characteristics (blemishes). Diagram is an approximate representation of the diamond, and symbols shown indicate type, position, and approximate size of clarity characteristics. All clarity characteristics may not be shown. Details of finish are not shown. The recipient of this Report may wish to consult a credentialed Jeweler or Gemologist about the importance and interrelationship of cut, color, clarity and carat weight.

IMPORTANT DOCUMENT, STORE SAFELY

8. The Ideal Cut Diamond — The Best and the Brightest

There had been disagreement on the exact specifications and tolerances of an ideal cut diamond until the last few years. Opinion in the trade has now fastened on the AGS definition as *The* ideal cut diamond.

This is because the AGS recently established a grading laboratory that certifies diamond quality and gives a cut grade, which the GIA lab does not. Also, an instrument that automatically measures every angle of every facet of a diamond and gives a printout with the AGS grade for each component of proportion has come into widespread use. This machine is called a Sarin machine (Sarin is only one brand, but it's come to be used generically.)

The AGS certificate and the Sarin machine have now made it routine to assess cut. A Sarin machine printout for a diamond is generally available for the asking from diamond wholesalers.

Before, since a GIA certificate does not give a cut grade (and only gives the table size and total depth), and the only instrument to measure angles was cumbersome and expensive (a manually operated shadowgraph), cut was a fuzzier concept and tended to be overlooked in favor of color and clarity. In fact the only practical way to assess cut was to estimate proportions visually.

AGS IDEAL CUT DIAMOND

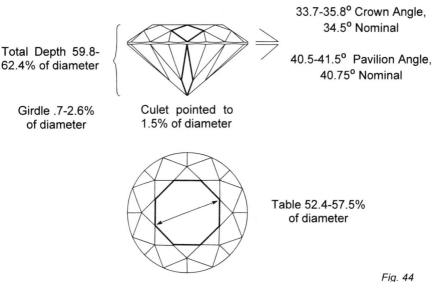

33.7-35.8° Crown Angle, 34.5° Nominal

Total Depth 59.8-62.4% of diameter

40.5-41.5° Pavilion Angle, 40.75° Nominal

Girdle .7-2.6% of diameter

Culet pointed to 1.5% of diameter

Table 52.4-57.5% of diameter

Fig. 44

Sarin Machine Report

WEIGHT	0.730	Ct,	
DIAMETER(mm)	5.834 (5.81 - 5.86) [0.8%]		
TOTAL DEPTH	% 61.6	3.59mm	
CROWN ANGLE	° 34.7 (34.4 - 34.9)		0
CROWN HEIGHT	% 15.2 (14.5 - 15.7)		0
PAVIL ANGLE	° 41.2 (40.5 - 41.9)		0
PAVIL DEPTH	% 43.6 (42.8 - 44.3)		0
CULET	% 0.5 V.Small		0
TABLE SIZE	% 56.3 (55.8 - 56.8)		0
GIRDLE THICKNESS	1.4 % (0.9-2.0)		0
	Medium		
PROPORTION	0		

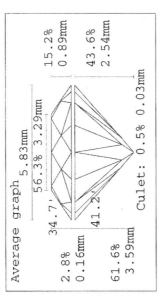

Average graph

5.83mm
56.3% 3.29mm
15.2% 0.89mm
34.7°
41.2°
43.6% 2.54mm
2.8% 0.16mm
61.6% 3.59mm
Culet: 0.5% 0.03mm

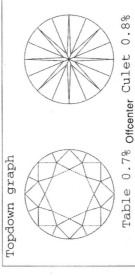

Topdown graph

Table 0.7% Offcenter Culet 0.8%

AGS	GOOD	V.G	EXC.	IDEAL	EXC.	V.G	GOOD
C.Angle	29.7 31.2	32.2 32.7	33.7 35.8	36.3 36.8	37.8 39.3		
C.Height	0.0 0.0	0.0 14.4	16.2 99.0	99.9 99.0			
P.Angle	0.0 39.0	40.0 40.5	41.5 42.4	43.0 44.0	99.0		
P.Depth	40.2 41.2	41.7 42.2	42.2 43.8	44.3 44.8	45.3 46.8		
Culet	0.0 0.0	0.0 0.0	1.5 3.8	4.6 5.1	99.0		
Table	49.4 49.4	50.4 52.3	52.4 57.5	58.5 65.5	69.5 71.5		
T.Depth	0.0 56.9	56.9 58.0	59.8 62.4	63.8 63.8	70.1 99.0		
Girdle	0.0 0.0	0.0 0.0	0.7 2.6	3.2 5.9	6.0 99.0		

Fig. 45

The AGS cut grading system is not a brilliance grade. It assumes that the original 1919 Tolkowsky cut, modified to allow some tolerance, is the best, and deducts for deviations from it. A diamond is graded for proportions, symmetry, and polish. An AGS ideal cut diamond has no deductions, or a 0 for each category, and is called a triple zero.

In the Sarin machine report on the previous page, you'll notice that there are zeros next to each measurement. This diamond scores an AGS grade of 0 for proportions.

AGS Ideal Proportions

Crown Angle °	33.7 – 35.8
Pavilion Angle °	40.5 – 41.5
Table % Diameter	52.4 – 57.5
Total Depth % Diameter	59.8 – 62.4
Girdle % Diameter	.7 – 2.6 (thin-slightly thick)
Culet % Diameter	0 (pointed) – 1.5

Crown height and pavilion depth are omitted from this table since they are determined by the table and angles and are just another expression of them.

But the machine can't grade symmetry and polish. That has to be done by humans, since it is subjective. And the only humans that can give an AGS grade are AGS humans. The GIA and other laboratories grade symmetry and polish, but can't guarantee that the AGS will agree with them. Since the only lab giving a cut grade is the AGS, a triple zero can only be given by the AGS. A GIA certificate with excellent grades for symmetry and polish accompanied by a Sarin report with a zero AGS grade for proportions does not guarantee a triple zero. (The GIA is promising more cut information on its certificates, though not a cut grade, by 2003.)

Diamond wholesalers and cutters tell me that obtaining an AGS ideal symmetry grade is an excruciating business, with the diamond sometimes having to be sent back to the cutter for minute touch-ups. Perhaps AGS standards for symmetry are tighter than those of the GIA.

Generally, the only reason to specifically obtain an AGS certificate is so that a diamond can be called a triple zero. I've already explained in great detail how proportions affect the brilliance of a diamond. In my opinion, symmetry variations within reasonable grades do not. A Sarin report with a zero proportion grade accompanying a diamond with a GIA certificate with very good or excellent grades for polish and symmetry costs the same at wholesale as a diamond with a triple zero AGS certificate. The market is saying that it doesn't matter because the differences are so minute.

But, since the price is the same, you'd want an AGS triple zero anyway. Why not? It doesn't cost any more. Well, ideal cuts aren't that easy to come by, especially when you're looking within a narrow range of size, color, and clarity. Many times I've called suppliers for a diamond of a specific size and quality and it's not in stock. And the GIA lab is much bigger than the AGS lab so there are many more diamonds with GIA certificates than AGS certificates. And certificates cost money, too much to have both a GIA and AGS certificate.

Hearts and Arrows

Believe it or not, there's yet another step up in symmetry: the hearts and arrows diamond. Diamond firms have been marketing "Hearts and Arrows" round diamonds. When a hearts and arrows diamond is viewed through a special device, reflections of the pavilion main facets form a pattern of spokes tipped with arrows when the diamond is viewed from the top. Eight hearts, each

Hearts and Arrows
Viewer

Fig. 46   Bottom view: hearts   Top view: arrows

Fig. 47

49

formed from 6 different facets, are seen around the diamond when it is viewed from the bottom.

The hearts and arrows viewer is quite simple. It consists of a lens suspended by three rods in a triangular configuration about four inches above the diamond, which is placed in the base of the instrument. Between the rods is a tube of yellow or orange plastic. The diamond is viewed through this tube. The colored plastic mutes the diamond's sparkle and somehow shades the facets so that the pattern of the facets jumps out to the eye as hearts and arrows.

What this device does is to demonstrate the perfection of symmetry of the diamond. The eye is very sensitive to slight imperfections of pattern and will detect a very slight misalignment of the facets or if the facets are slightly different in size or shape.

Does a hearts and arrows diamond look better than an ideal with very good or excellent symmetry or an AGS triple zero? I don't think you'd be able to tell the difference, although the hearts and arrows people will say otherwise. An indication that the market agrees with me is that the hearts and arrows diamonds I've bought didn't cost more than other ideals I've bought.

Let's kick it up another notch. There are branded ideal cuts that claim to be superior even to hearts and arrows diamonds. The claim is that they have perfect symmetry in three dimensions; that is, not only do all facets have the same shape and size and line up perfectly with each other, but they all have exactly the same angle, too. (If you look at the Sarin report on page 47, you'll see that the crown and pavilion angles are actually averages of the angles of each facet, with the range given in parentheses.)

These diamonds are accompanied by measurements of the diamond's brilliance via proprietary instruments, sort of shine-o-meters. These diamonds carry stiff premiums over other ideals. But the instruments they use are not available for others to test and have not been evaluated objectively by the GIA, which has the last word in these matters. And no one has lined up all the various brands and regular ideal cuts for a blind looking, as it were.

There are other parameters of diamond cut that are not included in grading by anyone yet and are not specified or graded by the AGS system: the star facets, and upper and lower girdle facets.

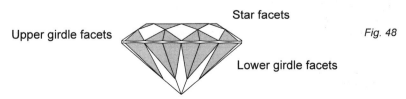

Upper girdle facets

Star facets

Lower girdle facets

Fig. 48

The lower girdle facets take up 80% of the pavilion surface area (as diamonds are usually cut; this can vary with their length) and the stars and upper and lower girdle facets 40% of the crown. Overall, these neglected facets take up over half of the diamond real estate. Computer modeling by the GIA indicates that their dimensions matter somewhat for brilliance and more significantly for dispersion. I suspect that differences in these may be more important than the last tiny bit of symmetry.

Nearly Ideal: The 60/60

When I want a diamond that is just off of an ideal cut I ask for a 60/60, meaning approximately a 60% table and 60% total depth. The 60% total depth is an indication that the stone isn't too shallow or deep or the girdle too thick, and the 60% table excludes the spread stones, diamonds that are deliberately cut with a large table to increase the diameter. It is possible for a literal 60/60 to have bad angles and poor brilliance, since only the table and depth are specified, but in practice 60/60 means a near ideal with angles that give good brilliance.

I have in my case now a .71 carat H VS1 diamond with a Sarin machine printout that has all zeros except for the table, which is 59.2% instead of the AGS ideal maximum of 57.5%.[8] The difference between 57.5% and 59.2% for this diamond would be only 1/10th of a millimeter, about 1/4 the width of the period at the end of this sentence. Yet this diamond sells for 15% less than an ideal. And I defy you to tell the difference in appearance. Of course, not every 60/60 is such a nearly ideal near-ideal. You may find some other minor variations in proportions. But if you work at it, you may very well be able to get a diamond that looks as good as an ideal for a lot less.

The Digital Diamond

The fly in the ideal cut ointment is the GIA's new computer model that analyzes brilliance and dispersion for round diamonds. This

---

8. Its GIA certificate on p.44 gives it a 60% table. I often see differences between GIA measurements and Sarin machine measurements. One diamond I saw was given a 58% table by the GIA and a 57% table by the machine, a difference between a 0 and a 1 AGS proportion grade. I would tend to believe the machine, but I would like to see a study of men vs. Machine. The GIA really should look into this.

model is a complicated three dimensional ray-tracing program that tracks all light rays that go into and out of a diamond.

The angles and dimensions of all the facets of a theoretical perfectly symmetrical diamond are fed into the computer and the result is a computer image of the patterns of light and dark that are seen when looking into a diamond. These virtual diamonds have a general correspondence to photos of actual diamonds of the same proportions under similar lighting conditions.

A light return percentage is also calculated, weighted to increasingly discount light the more off the vertical, and away from the eye, it exits the diamond.

The surprise is that diamonds with other, very different, proportions are calculated to have as much, or even more, light return than the traditional ideal cut. Some of these diamonds had larger tables, deeper pavilions, and crowns so shallow, down to 23°, that they're almost never encountered in the market. Others had proportions that were more in the normal range. The computer results were validated by observing a number of actual diamonds cut to both ideal and these different, but equally brilliant, proportions.

Similar results were found when dispersion was modeled: some diamonds with unconventional proportions were found to have high dispersion.

The GIA found that diamonds with certain combinations of very low crown angles, from 24° to 32°, with pavilion angles ranging from a shallow 38° to a steep 42° gave both good brilliance and fire as did diamonds with crown angles with the wide range of 20° to 36° and normal pavilion angles of 40° to 41°. An ideal cut diamond falls within the latter range.

These results also validate the experience of many in the trade of seeing an occasional diamond that is very brilliant yet deviates markedly from the traditional ideal cut. I once saw a diamond that had been recut with a 53% table but with a low crown angle comment on the accompanying GIA certificate. It was one of the most brilliant and fiery diamonds I've ever seen.

The AGS cut grading system deducts for deviations from each proportion element separately and also gives the same weight to deviations from each proportion element even though, as we have seen, small variations in pavilion angle are far more detrimental than in crown angle or table size.

The GIA computer model found that it is combinations of pavilion angle, crown angle, and table size acting together that determines light return. Moreover, combinations of them that give high brilliance were found to vary in complex ways that are difficult to systematize.

The implication is that you could buy a diamond as brilliant as an ideal cut for considerably less, since diamonds are discounted for cut based on deviations from AGS ideal proportions, not visual observation.

But there is no way to systematize visual observation of brilliance. There would be instant and cacophonous disagreement from various sectors of the diamond trade should that be attempted. And so powerful is the pressure for a cut grading system simple enough to be explained to the consumer that, for now, the AGS cut grading system remains in force. The grass may be greener on the other side of the fence, but no one has figured out how to climb the fence yet.

Your dilemma is that it would be up to you to spot the odd "off-make" diamond that is as brilliant and fiery as an ideal, and ideals are very brilliant and fiery, without seeing it next to an ideal for comparison.

We've all had the experience of seeing something that looked great yesterday, but not so hot today. With an ideal cut diamond you're mathematically guaranteed to have a very brilliant diamond, even if you're tired or in a bad mood.

Are you confused yet? Lots of angles and other technical business, and all you want is a pretty diamond. Well, if you walk into a Fifth Avenue type store, you can get one without any brainwork. But you'll have to pay for it. Somehow, I got on the mailing list of one of those internationally famous New York Fifth Avenue stores, as a consumer, not as a jeweler. It's pretty hard to evaluate complex jewelry from a picture, but one item was easy: a ½ carat round diamond in a plain 18 karat gold ring. Gotcha! 3 time mark-up. We purveyors of jewels to the unrich and unfamous would be lucky to get half of that.

What to Look For

If there's any problem with the angles of a diamond, it'll usually show up in the center. Look directly at the center of the diamond under bright lights. Yes, diamonds are shown under lights; you can't have light coming out of a diamond unless you have light going into a diamond. It's not a sales trick.

If the center area looks dark, the bottom is too steep. This is common. Refer the the photos on pages 31-33. You can see these reflections with the unaided eye. If the center looks dead, light gray with no sparkle, the bottom is too shallow. You may have a fisheye. But keep the diamond level. If you tilt a diamond with a correct pavilion angle you'll see the reflection of the girdle on one side. In a fisheye it forms a ring with the diamond level. If you see a curious lack of brilliance from the crown facets around the table, the crown is too steep.

You should see a uniform brilliance across the diamond from edge to edge. Tilt the diamond. The brilliance should be good from a variety of angles. Look at the diamond away from the lights. It should still be alive. Look again for darkness of weakness in the center.

Back under the lights. Move the diamond around and look for fire, flashes of different colors. You should see plenty of it. The fire will be mostly on the facets around the table, with a little from the center if you tilt the diamond. The diamond should look like a pool of light, almost without a distinct edge.

Look at the girdle. You'll be able to spot a thick girdle with the eye, although you may have trouble seeing a knife-edge girdle without magnification. Thin, but not knife-edge, girdles look pretty thin to the unaided eye.

Move the diamond until you get the flash from the table. You'll be able to see from this if it's overly large. Refer to the photos on page 35. It may be difficult to see the bowing business with the eye, but you'll see it under the microscope. And, of course, it's unprofessional for a seller of diamonds not to have a microscope.

OK, you've passed looking 101. Now it's time for the field trip. A good way to start would be to go see a no-fooling-around ideal cut round diamond. Not every store carries these premium diamonds. It should be no problem, though, to see mediocre or poorly cut stones. There are plenty of them out there. Go to different types of stores and see a variety of diamonds. Practice your looking skills.

But remember, you're still novice lookers. Some people catch on right away, and others aren't sure of themselves, or are too suggestible: they'll see what the salesman says they ought to see. Still others see what isn't there. I've had people swear they could see color differences that I sure couldn't. We are prisoners of our personalities.

It will be easy to spot the badly cut diamonds. Everyone has a story about someone showing off her large, ugly rock. But you'll also see a lot of borderline stones. Borderline round diamonds will typically have larger tables, 62-64%, and be a little deep on the bottom and a little dark in the center and maybe a little steep on the top. And they'll look pretty good. But side-by-side with an ideal cut, you'll immediately see the difference. But you probably won't get to see the two side-by-side.

I once did an appraisal on a ¾ carat diamond that had the worst proportions imaginable. It was a fisheye stone, so shallow on the bottom that the white ring of the girdle reflection was visible under the table, and the crown was at least 45°. But the diamond didn't look too bad – just a little weak in the center. Some wily cutter found an extreme way to compensate for the shallow pavilion. I couldn't believe it looked as good as it did, so I ran it through my computer model and, sure enough, it came out not too bad. You could be fooled by a diamond like this. If it were for sale, I'm sure it would be incredibly cheap and you might want to buy it. But you should know what you're buying.

The best way to avoid inadvertently settling for second-best is to choose only from among well-cut diamonds. At some point an ideal slides over into a 60/60 that looks the same because something's off just a little. But at some point it doesn't look the same because something's off too much. Finding that point is the trick.

Spotting one of those diamonds with unconventional proportions that the GIA found to be as bright as an ideal will probably be a matter of chance. These revelations by the GIA are too new and unsystematic to give rise to wholesalers who would specialize in them or cutters who would make them purposely rather than as a matter of necessity. And acceptance by the conservative and tradition-bound world of diamond dealers would have to await strong demand from the market.

Most off-make diamonds aren't pretty. Most jewelers who carry off-makes, don't carry fine cuts also, and vice-versa. This is where finding a jeweler you can trust comes in. Turn up the sensitivity on your crap detector and find your own comfort level. And sort out what your head wants versus what your eyes can see.

9. Fancy Shape Diamonds

Diamonds that aren't round are fancy shapes. There is no ideal cut for fancy shapes and no one has modeled them on a computer; they're too complicated. You're on your own. You have to judge by looking. But you should still watch out for overly deep or shallow stones, very large tables, especially in the square or rectangular shapes, and thick or knife-edge girdles.

The same general principles hold for fancy shapes as for rounds: pavilion and crown angles determine light return and brilliance. But these angles must necessarily vary to accommodate their shapes. For instance, the pavilion facets at the sides of a marquise have to be steeper than those at the points since they all slope to meet at the same place, the culet.

Even the number of pavilion main facets can vary from the standard 8. Marquises can have 6 or 8 and pears can have 5,7, or 9. I once had a shallow pear-shaped diamond recut to improve brilliance. The cutter put only 4 main facets on the pavilion and added extra lower girdle facets on the bottom of the point. This was unconventional, but the stone was a knockout. Sometimes small extra facets are put on the crown near the points This is called a French tip. All this variation affects the look of the diamond, the balance of appearance from the center to the point, and scintillation.

With pears and marquises, the first thing to look for is bow-tie, a dark area across the center of the stone shaped like a bow-tie. Bow-tie is perfectly obvious, and yet I've seen many consumers who did not notice it until it was pointed out to them. Or maybe they thought it was supposed to look that way. Well, it isn't supposed to look that way. This speaks not to having a trained eye, but to a freezing of the mind. It doesn't take a trained eye to see that the emperor has no clothes.

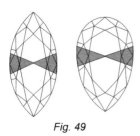

Fig. 49

Fig. 50

Bow-tie

56

Even a fine marquise or pear may be a little weak in the center or have a faint bow-tie. These elongated stones don't have the symmetrical brilliance of a round. Scintillation is the hallmark of these cuts. Even brilliance and scintillation across these stones is difficult to achieve. You should watch out for displeasing differences in appearance between the center and the points.

Very wide tables and shallow crowns are common on pears and marquises. The tables on these stones are measured corner-to-corner across the width of the diamond, not the length, and table percentages are calculated by dividing the table width by the width of the diamond. Table sizes will probably be larger than for rounds, but should be under, say, 62%.

You should also watch out for dead stones. This may seem like a no-brainer, but I see plenty of pears and marquises that are simply dead, usually because they are too shallow, just slivers. Someone thought they looked good when they were purchased. Don't let that someone be you.

Ovals should be close to rounds in brilliance, although they may also have bow-tie. Hearts and princess cuts, not being elongated, should also have even brilliance like a round diamond.

Shape is a consideration for all elongated diamonds. Too fat, too thin, or blocky-looking stones are common in pears, marquises, and ovals. Generally, the desirable length-to-width ratio for marquises is 1.75-2 to 1, and for pears, emeralds, and ovals about 1.5 to 1. But mainly the shape should be pleasing to the eye.

Calibration is also a factor. Heads, the settings with the prongs that hold diamonds, are made to fit the nominal sizes of various diamond weights. If a diamond is too fat or too thin, it will be a trial to set it in a head that really doesn't fit. You may end up with a diamond that is poorly set or prongs that have been cut too thin for security.

Emerald cuts (rectangles with beveled corners) are not brilliant cuts; they are step cuts. They have even rows of parallel facets and

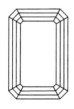 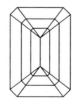  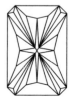

Fig. 51 The emerald cut is a step cut.

The radiant is a brilliant cut. *Fig. 52*

not a point on the bottom, but a keel line. They have an icy look rather than a sparkly look, and little fire. However, there is a brilliant cut rectangular diamond called a radiant cut. The radiant cut has sparkle and scintillation that the emerald cut does not. If you're thinking of an emerald cut, sort out in your mind whether you want the tailored, icy look of an emerald cut or just the rectangular shape. If the latter, consider a radiant cut. There is also a square radiant cut. Which should be considered along with princess and other square cuts discussed below.

There are also other, branded, rectangular brilliant cuts, with different faceting than a radiant. As with all branded cuts, they sell at a premium and can have limited distribution.

Emerald cuts should be higher in clarity than the other cuts. You can see right into the stone and inclusions that would be masked by the sparkle of the brilliant cuts may be visible in an emerald cut.

Emerald cuts and princess cuts are frequently all bottom and no top. Very wide tables, 70-80%, and very small and shallow crowns are common. Emerald cuts can also bulge out on the bottom, adding useless weight.

Princess cuts are a bit of fad now for engagement rings. Personally, I think they look clunky as center stones when they're set high off a ring like most engagement rings. I think they look much better in a low setting, especially with trillions on either side for a geometric look. You should consider today's look versus a classic style. Fashions come and go, but a classic, like a diamond, is forever.

There is a Canadian diamond company, Sirius Diamonds, offering what they call an ideal cut princess, that they say has the same brilliance as a round diamond.

There are also square diamonds with beveled corners, unlike a princess which has pointed corners. The most famous is offered by Tiffany, called the Lucida. It is a patented 50 facet square cut, recently offered in a rectangular version, originally called the Flanders cut.

A diamond company in Chicago offers a square or rectangular cut also said to equal a round in brilliance called the Lucere, which comes in two versions: the mixed cut American Lucere with a step cut crown and brillianteered pavilion, and the European Lucere, which is a brilliant cut. The Lucere has 65 facets. The Asscher cut, a very deep square step cut with a small table, is enjoying a revival now after a hundred years, being especially popular in Hollywood. However, an Asscher cut will be very small for its weight.

In fact, there is a proliferation of patented diamond cuts of every shape, inspired by the industry's newfound obsession with cut and ideal cuts. A recent article in *Gems & Gemology*, the GIA's quarterly journal, lists 81 patented diamond cuts. There are even patented variants of the round diamond with more facets, or different faceting patterns. One has 100 facets and only 12 are manufactured a year.

Patented and branded diamonds usually carry premiums and won't live at your local jeweler. Generally, they are carried by upscale jewelers who participate in the wholesalers' marketing programs. But similar generic versions are available.

10. Small Diamonds — Diamonds for a Dollar

Small diamonds, used in cluster settings, band rings, and as accent stones, are miniature versions of larger diamonds. They're not "chips", whatever that is. They are called *melee* ("melly"). Grading for melee is less stringent than for larger diamonds. The VVS, VS, and SI clarity grades are not subdivided into categories 1 and 2. Color is given in ranges, i.e., D-F, G-H. While crown and pavilion angles should be correct, small diamonds usually have thicker girdles, and the details of the cut, such as facets meeting at a point, are not given the same attention as with larger stones.

With engagement ring diamonds, say, 1/3 carat and above, the difference in price from low quality to high of what you will see will be about 1.5 times. But with melee it'll be over 10 times.

Nobody would buy a lifeless diamond if it were large enough to see its lifelessness up close and personal. But people buy jewelry with pretty awful little diamonds. Perhaps budget induces people to buy "bluff pieces", the look without the price. Or maybe a colored stone center distracts from its background. Whatever the reason, low quality "total weight" pieces are produced and sold by the bushel.

You've seen those multi-carat tennis bracelets or diamond hearts advertised for a few hundred dollars. What do you think you get for that kind of money? You get what one diamond dealer calls "deads" or "semi-deads", or what another calls "frozen spit." Some are so full of cracks they look white. Others are so full of black spots they look gray. Cutting on these diamonds was an afterthought. Some of these diamonds cost only a dollar each – retail.

Although I've seen worse in terms of clarity, the most astonishing melee piece was a tennis bracelet brought in for repair with 3 of its 10 point diamonds missing. The bracelet was 10 karat gold, a tip-off to low quality of itself. The diamonds were I2-I3 clarity, par for low price stones. But the astonishing part was how they were cut. Huge tables, small tables, crown angles approaching the vertical, fisheyes, nailheads.....a veritable museum of lapidary pathology. Needless to say, the diamonds had little brilliance. I can't imagine how low the price was for this 5 carat bracelet, but it must have been a record. The customer wisely chose to have the missing diamonds replaced with cubic zirconias, which stood out starkly from their dreary companions.

Small diamonds are supposed to be brilliant, too. A tennis bracelet should be a ribbon of light and a diamond heart should light up her eyes.

White, lower cost melee that is included, SI2-I1 clarity, but that is bright and shiny because it is well cut, can be used to reduce the cost of multi-carat pieces by 35-40% from higher clarity goods without sacrificing appearance. But it's difficult to find because it's harder to recover the costs of extra labor and waste involved in cutting lower price goods correctly.

You may hear the term "Russian cut" to refer to fine cut melee. In the old Soviet economy there was no pressure to cut costs, so the Russians simply, and inefficiently, cut diamonds correctly. Fine melee is also cut in low-wage Asian countries now. It takes a lot of labor to cut 50 stones to the carat. And there's less yield from the rough for fine cuts. This can only be offset by low costs.

Some small diamonds are cut automatically by machine. Israel is a pioneer in automation.

It's harder to find well-cut melee, even in higher color and clarity grades, than well-cut larger diamonds. Uniformity, although not as extreme as in the tennis bracelet example, is a problem. Diamonds that are deep and shallow, with thick and thin crowns and large and small tables will give an uneven appearance to a piece of jewelry: some diamonds will be bright and others won't. I once had a diamond dealer send me a "melange parcel", mixed sizes, of F or better color VVS clarity diamonds for inspection. These "collection goods" should have beeen knockouts. And they should have been expensive. But the price was too good to be true. A quick examination showed me why: perhaps 10% of the diamonds were well made, the rest were off willy-nilly.

In multi-carat jewelry with small diamonds, you should look for brilliance and uniformity – no dead stones. You will probably have to compromise on clarity. Those carats can add up and something has to give to make it affordable. Most tennis bracelets have SI2-I1 clarity diamonds to keep the cost down. This is all right if the diamonds are well-cut and bright. Look for the shine, but you might not want to look under a microscope.

In smaller items with total weights of a carat or under, such as a diamond heart, you should be able to get better diamonds without breaking the bank, although you may have to break the budget.

Diamond nameplates and initial rings often have pretty bad diamonds, perhaps because they're often destined for teenagers and budgets are more limited. And most of them have only a few small diamonds in each letter, rather than a continuous line. They're usually set in white gold which is "bright cut" and it all blends together so you won't notice the spaces between the diamonds.

Older jewelry, dating from the Sixties back, often has single-cut melee in sizes .01-.04 carat (1.3-2.2mm). Single cuts have 17 facets rather than the 58 facets of full cuts. Actually, they ought to be called "half-cuts", since they are diamonds that have been blocked but not brillianteered. Occasionally, I see "promotional quality" contemporary jewelry set with single cuts. I'm sure they exist, but I've never seen bright, well-cut single-cut diamonds.

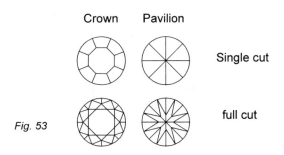

Crown   Pavilion

Single cut

full cut

Fig. 53

People generally realize that with engagement-size diamonds the price per carat depends on the size, that a 1 carat diamond costs more than twice as much as a half carat diamond. But they are unaware that there are size/price categories for small diamonds also. This can lead to misperceptions when comparison shopping. For example, 10 pointers (.10 carat) cost about 25% more than 1 to 7 pointers (.01-.07 carat) of the same quality. And 20 pointers cost more than 15 pointers. Keep this in mind when comparing two items of the same total weight.

Nominal Sizes For Small Diamonds

.01	.02	.03	.05	.07	.10	.15	.20	Carat	
o	o	○	○	○	○	○	○		
1.3	1.7	2.0	2.4	2.7	3.0	3.4	3.8	MM	*Fig. 54*

Although rounds are the usual choice for melee, small marquises and pear shapes are also used. The same criteria apply as for solitaires: good brilliance and no bow-tie. I've seen marquise band rings in which all the bow-ties lined up along the center of the ring, forming a dark line. Their owners seemed unaware of it until it was pointed out to them.

Princess cuts are popular for accent stones on the shoulders of engagement rings, usually channel-set. In channel-setting, the diamonds are set almost touching each other in a groove. The groove is actually smaller than the diamonds. The diamonds are set by cutting a notch in one side of the channel below the rim with a bur using a flexible shaft machine (like a Dremel tool). When the notch is deep enough, the diamonds can be slipped into the channel. The metal is then hammered over the diamonds using the flexible shaft fitted with a reciprocating rather than a rotary bit. A notch in the opposite channel wall locks the diamonds in place. Princess cut diamonds are also commonly channel-set. Channel-setting gives a sleek look versus the lacy look of prongs.

Princess cuts are used exclusively in invisible setting. Invisible setting involves setting two or more rows of princess cuts edge to edge in a channel with no metal showing between the diamonds. To do this, grooves are cut into the diamonds below the girdle. The grooves fit into metal ribs in the mounting. The edge and end diamonds are channel-set in the usual manner – the metal of the channel walls is hammered over the edges of the diamonds. The effect is of an unbroken diamond surface.

Baguettes are small rectangular diamonds that are usually at least twice as long as they are wide. Tapered baguettes are narrower on one end and straight baguettes are the same width at each end. Tapered baguettes are often used as accents on either side of a solitaire diamond. They can also be used to create an arc, by lining them up with the small ends in.

Baguettes are step-cuts, with rows of parallel facets running around the stone, not brilliant cuts. Baguettes are emerald cuts without the bevels on the corners. Baguettes need to be cleaner than round diamonds since they are less brilliant and inclusions, especially dark ones, would be more noticeable. Baguettes and invisible-set princess cuts are the most expensive of the small diamonds.

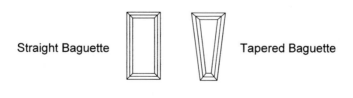

Straight Baguette   Tapered Baguette

Fig. 55

11. Enhancements – Doctoring Diamonds

All black onyx and blue topaz on the market owes its color to laboratory treatment. "Black onyx" does occur naturally in the black and white banded agate properly called onyx, but it is not commercially feasible to cut out the black bands.

The black onyx you see everywhere comes out of the ground as a grayish material of the same composition (a form of quartz called chalcedony, pronounced kal-séduhny) as the naturally colored gem. It is then boiled in a sugar solution and soaked in acid to turn it black. This has been done since antiquity (they used honey then). Blue topaz starts out as natural colorless topaz, which is abundant and occurs in large crystals. It is irradiated, under license from the Nuclear Regulatory Commission, and then heated to produce the blue color. Natural blue topaz is rare and much paler. Most other colored stones are enhanced in some fashion.

Diamonds are also doctored, but not as commonly as colored stones. Federal Trade Commission regulations require that gemstone enhancements be disclosed to the buyer. You owners of black onyx and blue topaz jewelry know that this disclosure requirement is not carried out. Does this bother you? Probably not too much. Would it bother you to know that your engagement ring diamond was doctored?

Laser-drilling of diamonds is done to improve clarity. A hair-fine channel is drilled with a laser to reach a piqué, a black eye-visible inclusion. The inclusion is then dissolved out, improving the appearance of the diamond and transforming an I clarity stone to a much more saleable SI clarity.

I've seen a number of laser-drilled diamonds brought in by customers for evaluation or jewelry repair. In no case had the customer been informed that their diamond was "clarity-enhanced". One such stone, lasered in three places, had been purchased at a major department store. Another had been sold to the consumer by a diamond wholesaler as a favor. Laser-drilling is easily seen under the microscope.

In another process, fractures that reach the surface of the diamond are filled with a glass whose refractive index (see footnote on page 27) is near to that of diamond. This eliminates the contrast between the diamond and the air-filled fracture, which appears white, and it disappears from view, rather like cracks in an ice cube that disappear once it is put in water.

Filled diamonds are detected under the microscope by characteristic flashes of colors as the filled fracture is viewed end-on. This is caused by a mismatch in dispersion between the diamond and the glass filling. I once saw a filled diamond in which, due to the orientation of the fracture, an eye-visible hot pink flash was seen face-up, continuously. At first I thought it was fingernail polish on the bottom of the diamond (although it was a man's ring). It took me a while to figure it out.

Sometimes diamonds are both drilled and filled. If the the fracture to be filled doesn't reach the surface, a hole is drilled down to it so that it can be filled. This also fills the drill holes. One drilled and filled diamond I saw had rainbow colors emanating from the drill holes under the microscope.

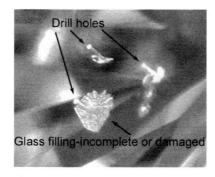

Fig. 56

This diamond has been drilled in three places and one of the resulting cavities has been filled. The glass filling was either incomplete or has been damaged, possibly by ultrasonic cleaning.The customer was unaware that her diamond had been doctored.

Filled diamonds still have relatively low clarity, so don't get too paranoid about it in better diamonds.

This process has stability problems. The glass filling will not survive the heating involved in certain repairs, such as retipping the prongs with the diamond in place. Also, there have been reports of the filling material degrading with ultrasonic cleaning and simulated exposure to sunlight.

Fracture-filled diamonds are out there in force according to the trade press and there was a TV exposé of a St. Louis jeweler who sold filled diamonds without disclosure in 1993. The wholesalers of these diamonds take out full page ads in jewelry trade magazines. But I've only seen a few brought in by unwary customers. The GIA will not grade fracture-filled or laser-drilled diamonds.

There's a new process in which the color of one type of diamond is permanently improved. Brown diamonds of a certain rare type, in which color is caused by atomic structural defects in the crystal rather than nitrogen impurities, are most susceptible to the process. The treatment involves high temperature and pressure. Diamonds can be treated either rough or cut, although the cut diamonds have to be repolished after such a severe treatment. The treatment is permanent and the treated diamonds are indistinguishable to the eye from untreated diamonds of the same color.

The process was developed by General Electric, the inventor of synthetic diamonds, and revealed in 1999. The diamonds, which are treated before they are cut, are distributed by Pegasus Overseas Limited, a subsidiary of Lazare Kaplan International. This is amusing because Lazare Kaplan heretofore was the ultimate diamond purist, assuming the Tolkowsky mantle with the first brand-name ideal cut diamond. In 2000, these color-enhanced diamonds were branded "Bellataire".

Lazare Kaplan has agreed to laser-inscribe on the girdle of all treated diamonds "GE POL" in tiny letters, and not to sell treated rough to other cutters. However, just a few months after these treated diamonds went on sale in 1999, the GIA received treated diamonds to grade that had had the inscriptions polished off. The diamonds were detected because they had initially been submitted with the inscriptions, and were matched through computer records. The policy of the GIA in such cases is to require that the diamonds be re-inscribed or the incident be reported to industry watchdog organizations. The GIA will grade properly inscribed treated diamonds, but will note the treatment on the certificate.

This high temperature high pressure process has also be used to change the color of the more common type of brown diamond to yellow and green yellow. Pink and blue diamonds have also been made by this method.

Recently, a Michigan company began offering this type of color enhancement to the trade, treating rough diamonds submitted by others. Identification inscriptions would presumably be the responsibility of those others. The Russians, who are at the forefront of crystal synthesis, are also color-enhancing diamonds. It must be assumed that some treated diamonds are entering the market without disclosure.

Detection of this process requires pretty high tech equipment involving ultraviolet and infrared spectra, photoluminescence, cathodoluminescence, and cooling diamonds with liquid nitrogen –

stuff I don't do at the store. At this point the GIA feels that it can conclusively state that a diamond is *not* treated.

Some colored diamonds are irradiated to produce their colors. Very intensely colored diamonds are suspicious if they're not in a museum or jet-set milieu. Any green diamond is suspect.

Natural color diamonds, other than "champagne" and yellow diamonds, are take-your breath-away expensive. If you see a blue, orange, or pink diamond whose price doesn't have you gasping for air, beware.[9] The rule of thumb for pink diamond melee is 20 times the cost of comparable white diamonds.

Black diamonds are in vogue now, featured as melee mixed with white diamonds. Black diamonds are affordable, but many of the black diamond pieces I've seen had irradiated black diamonds, which was disclosed by the wholesaler. The black color in natural black diamonds is caused by a multitude of black inclusions in a white diamond. Irradiated black diamonds are turned greenish black throughout by irradiation, so the two are readily separated by visual inspection under a microscope.

Any natural color diamond, (brown and small yellow excepted) larger than tiny should come with a GIA certificate stating natural origin of color. Some pretty hoity-toity designer jewelry sports small irradiated diamonds in a variety of colors. They're affordable, and fun. I've been buying jewelry with small (melee to ¼ carat) natural yellow diamonds that is affordable. It seems there's more of this material on the market now. Larger sizes cost more than white, but are thinkable. If you see colored diamonds, always ask if the color is natural or irradiated.

Don't get too paranoid about all this. Doctored diamonds don't just pop up at random. They're sold through their own channels, and the vast majority of doctored diamonds are sold with disclosure. It's the few crooks that get the headlines. And a diamond with a certificate means that a gemological laboratory with far more resources than a retailer has vetted the diamond for treatments.

---

9. Red diamonds are the rarest, with only a handful known. The Hancock Red Diamond, .95 carat and with an eye-visible flaw, sold at auction in 1987 for $880,000, or $926,000 per carat.

12. Simulants and Synthetics — Fakes and Real Fakes

A synthetic, or man-made (or "created"), gem *is* the gem, made in the laboratory instead of the earth. It has the same chemical structure and physical properties as the natural gemstone. There are usually minor characteristics that enable the gemologist to separate the synthetic from the natural.

A simulant is a gem, natural or man-made, that is used to imitate another gem. Colorless zircon[10], synthetic spinel, Fabulite (strontium titanate), YAG (yttrium aluminum garnet), glass, and other materials have been used as imitation diamonds.

These have been superseded by the popular man-made diamond simulant cubic zirconia[11]. Cubic zirconia was invented in Russia in the 1970's. Initially sold by the carat, this imitation is now so widespread that I sell a 1 carat diamond size CZ for $5, and feel a little guilty at the profit.

Cubic zirconia, with a refractive index, the measure of a material's ability to bend light and thereby its potential for brilliance, of about 2.15, is a brilliant stone. But not as brilliant as diamond with a refractive index of 2.417. Side-by-side, you will be able to tell a cz from a diamond. I have run this experiment with customers, and it works.

Cubic zirconia, however, has more fire (dispersion) than diamond. With a hardness higher than most gems, but below that of ruby and sapphire, it is durable. But it does not approach the incomparable hardness of diamond.

A quick way to tell cz from diamond is to lay the stone upside-down over print. You will be able to see distorted print through the cz, but nothing through the diamond. (Caution – this may not work with diamonds that aren't round.) This is a direct observation of light leaking out the bottom of a cz through its 13% larger critical angle escape window, carrying the image of the print with it. Another quick way to tell cz from diamond is to have it measured

---

10. Don't confuse zircon, a natural gemstone, and December's birthstone, with cubic zirconia, the man-made diamond imitation. The former is natural zirconium silicate and the latter is man-made zirconium oxide, with added stabilizers. Although colorless zircons have been used in the past as diamond imitations, zircon occurs in a variety of colors with light blue (artificially colored by heating) being the most common. Zircon has a very high refractive index of 1.98, so it is very bright. However, it is not a happy ring stone. It is easily abraded and will eventually get a sandpapered look.

11. The cubic business refers to the crystal structure of the zirconia, or zirconium oxide. Diamond is cubic carbon. Hexagonal carbon is graphite.

and weighed. Cubic zirconia is a lot heavier than diamond. People are always coming in with stones they found in a parking lot and want to know if they're diamonds. I can tell by looking, but the weight demonstration gets their attention. I measure the stone and tell them what it would weigh if it were a diamond, then put it on the scale and show them how much more it weighs. So far, the parking lot score is cubic zirconia 100, diamond 1. This high ratio of lost and found fake to real is probably due to cubic zirconia being set in cheesier rings, but I do wonder where all the lost diamonds go.

You can ignore claims that this or that brand of cz (or "diamonique") is better. They're all white and flawless these days. The only difference is the cutting, and they're all cut pretty well, too. Cubic zirconia is now a standard commodity product.

The latest entry into the fake diamond market is synthetic silicon carbide, called synthetic moissanite after French chemist Henri Moissan, who discovered natural silicon carbide grains in Meteor Crater, near Winslow, Arizona in 1893. They were made by the impact of the meteor, 50,000 years ago.

You know silicon carbide as carborundum, a synthetic industrial abrasive that has been manufactured for 100 years. Making black grit is one thing and making large colorless crystals is another. But it has recently been accomplished by a North Carolina firm, initially called 3C, now styled as Charles and Colvard.

Synthetic moissanite is the most believable diamond imitation yet. It has a higher refractive index than diamond, but visually its brilliance was judged slightly less than diamond by the GIA. This is probably due to its strong double refraction: it belongs to a class of crystals that split entering light into two rays, each of which takes a separate path through the stone. This gives it a fuzzier brilliance. However, in crystals of this type, there is one direction through the stone that does not split light, called the optic axis, and moissanite is cut so that you're looking in that direction with the stone face-up. This eliminates the fuzzy effect in the most important view.

This property of double refraction provides a key to identifying moissanite, since double images of the back facets and culet are seen when looking into the stone at an angle through the kite-shaped crown main facets. Diamond does not have double images.

Double refraction can also be confirmed with an instrument called a polariscope, a small basic instrument, along with a microscope, that any store with a gemologist on staff should have. A polariscope enables one to view a gemstone in polarized light. When rotated under polarized light, gems of moissanite's class blink alternately light and dark. This only works for moissanite when the stone is held girdle up, since face-up or face-down presents the optic axis, the one direction in which the stone does not split light. Diamond stays dark when rotated under polarized light in any orientation.

Moissanite also has distinctive needle-like inclusions, sometimes in profusion, that are never seen in diamond. I haven't seen all that many moissanites, but I've never seen a stone without these inclusions.

Fig. 57

Fig. 58

Figs. 57, 58, 59, Characteristic needle-like inclusions in moissanite. Fig. 59, Note in the background the reflected double images of the inclusion under the table circled in fig. 57. Fig. 60, double images of the back facets and culet viewed through a crown main facet.

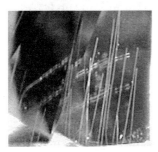

Fig. 59

Fig. 60

Moissanite shows a faint green or yellow tint, comparable to diamond color grades of J-K. This is not that noticeable when set in jewelry. (I once retipped a broken prong on a moissanite ring with the stone in place – like diamond moissanite can take the heat. The stone turned quite green when heated, then reverted to near-colorless when it cooled).

The unfaceted girdles of moissanite are distinctly different from the ground glass appearance of a diamond girdle. Moissanite is less dense than diamond. Two 6.5mm moissanites I set for earrings weighed .84 carat and .86 carat, versus about 1 carat for a diamond of the same size.

Moissanite has has more than twice the dispersion (fire) of diamond. As was explained before, fire increases with size in a gemstone. At around the one carat (diamond size – 6.5mm) mark, the fire in moissanite becomes very noticeable, too much for diamond. I can't say this is bad, just different.

Moissanite will fool a diamond testing instrument, which measures the ability of a material to conduct heat. These testing instruments are small hand-held devices with a pin-like tip that is pressed against the stone, and an LCD readout which will say "diamond" or "simulant". New testers based on electrical conductivity have come on the market which will detect moissanite.

At 9¼, moissanite has a hardness greater than corundum (ruby and sapphire), but still far less than diamond at 10.[12]

Initially (1999), the 3C company, now Charles and Colvard, was committed to a package program for moissanite, not selling single stones. A store had to stock a lot of it, display it with company literature, and generally get snooty about this pricey imitation. In a call to 3C in response to a customer request for moissanite, I was told I could buy a single stone, but at a price above wholesale. But they wouldn't tell me how much above wholesale, so I could price it fairly. (Taking 25% off the odd price per carat they quoted left a nice round number). They also told me they only had one store in all of New Jersey stocking moissanite (in Atlantic City).

Now, Charles and Colvard has abandoned the exclusive approach and sells moissanite through large distributors, enabling small stores to order stones as needed. All the distributors seem to be reading from the same price list, and the stuff ain't cheap. It seems to be pegged at about 10% of the price of a comparably sized diamond. You can expect to pay over $450 for a 1 carat diamond equivalent size moisssanite and $1100 for a 2 carat size. Pretty expensive for a fake. Maybe it'll go the way of cz prices in the future.

But not to worry. Real fake diamonds are coming soon. They've been coming soon for about 10 years, with bouts of coming sooner.

---

12. The Mohs hardness scale, devised by early 19th centery German mineralogist Friedrich Mohs, does not have uniform divisions. It arbitrarily defines 10 minerals as hardness standards, with talc at 1 and diamond at 10. Any mineral ranking higher will scratch one ranking lower. The hardness of corundum (ruby and sapphire), at 9, is much closer to topaz, at 8, than to diamond, at 10.

Synthetic diamonds were first made by General Electric in 1954. This was industrial diamond abrasive grit. It took pressures of over 400 tons per square inch and temperatures over 2500° F in a small chamber of a special press to do this.

Today synthetic diamond abrasive is made 30 carats at a press run, which only takes a few minutes. Over half of all industrial diamond abrasive is synthetic.

But making large gem-quality crystals is much more difficult. By the late 1960's GE researchers had learned to make large, clear crystals, usually colored yellow by nitrogen. But at great expense, taking days to grow them. Today large crystals, both yellow and colorless, are made for scientific and industrial uses, mostly by GE, DeBeers (see next chapter), Japan's Sumitomo Company, and Russian companies. It takes about 48 hours to grow a 1 carat diamond. So far they have not covertly entered the gem market, perhaps because they are, as of now, easily identified.

Synthetic diamonds have been intensely studied by the GIA and DeBeers, and are easily detected by laboratory techniques. Standard gemological equipment available in jewelry stores can detect many of them, under the microscope by distinctive inclusions, and by characteristic patterns displayed under polarized light and ultraviolet light. Many synthetic diamonds are attracted to a strong magnet due to metallic inclusions resulting from the method of manufacture. Uncut synthetic diamond crystals look totally different from the natural.

In 1994, the Chatham company, the inventor of synthetic emeralds in the 1930's, announced that it would be marketing synthetic diamonds made in Russia at a tenth the cost of natural diamonds. The Russians are the premier crystal growers of the world and the labor is very cheap. The initial production quantities were stated to be only 100 carats a month. A few were shown to the GIA, and then the project fizzled, a casualty of the chaos in post-Soviet Russia.

In the intervening years, other companies have stated the imminent arrival of gem-quality synthetic diamonds to the consumer market, made in Russia or Ukraine, at a third the price of natural diamonds.

A Florida company announced that in a few years it will be making 30-40,000 synthetic diamonds a year with 300 machines. Only yellow diamonds for now. Maybe real fake diamonds have gone from coming soon to coming sooner again.

13. DeBeers — The Syndicate

The DeBeers company of South Africa has monopoly control of world diamond markets and prices, the Darth Vader of diamonds. Diamonds are the only commodity so controlled. Microsoft would aspire to be the DeBeers of software.

DeBeers was founded by Cecil Rhodes (founder of Rhodesia, now Zimbabwe, and Rhodes scholarships) who bought up hundreds of small claims in the Kimberly mine, the first South African pipe mine, then swallowed his larger competitors in 1889, forming DeBeers Consolidated Mines. Control of other mines and then the diamond industry as a whole followed. Rhodes died in 1902. DeBeers was taken over by Ernest Oppenheimer, the founder of Anglo-American, a large gold-mining company, in 1926 and his family runs it today.

This highly secretive organization, still occasionally called The Syndicate, as it was known in the 19th century, controls every aspect of the diamond business and has substantial interests in gold and other minerals as well, via Anglo-American. DeBeers owns some diamond mines and has partnerships in others. But its contracts with diamond mines and governments of diamond mining countries to market most of their production had enabled DeBeers to control 85% of the rough diamond market, gem and industrial, until recently. Its share was down to 57% in 2001.

DeBeers hold "sights" 10 times a year in London to which a select group of diamond cutting firms and rough diamond dealers, called sightholders, are invited. DeBeers recently trimmed its list of sightholders to 120 from 200 as part of a major reorganization initiated a few years ago. These customers are given a box of rough diamonds on a take-it-or-leave-it basis. Leaving it is unwise. Stefan Kanfer[13] describes the experience of Harry Winston:

> Winston disliked this high-handed manner of diamond disposal (after all, didn't his clients include the Duke and Duchess of Windsor? the Arab emirates?).
> At one sight he handed back his box, walked out, and attempted to go around the syndicate, negotiating to buy rough diamonds from an independent firm in Angola, then a Portuguese possession. One phone call was made, from a British Cabinet member to a high official in Portugal. The Crown, the member said drily, would regard a deal between the colony and Mr. Winston as "an unfriendly act." Winston got the message. He never refused a box again.

13. The Last Empire, Farrar Straus & Giroux, 1993

While taking into account the sightholders' specializations within the diamond-cutting field and allowing some price negotiation on large rough, DeBeers dumps unwanted or difficult to cut rough diamonds by forcing their clients to take it. Should a producer, company or country, get out of line by trying to sell outside the "single channel marketing" system, DeBeers will flood the market with just the sort of diamonds the apostate mines from its $4.5 billion stockpile. Political influence is brought to bear when necessary, as seen in the Harry Winston example.

The prices for rough diamonds and thereby the polished diamonds you buy had been set by this monopoly. DeBeers raised prices 21% in 1989-90 and raised prices an average of 8.5% a year from 1975-1993. It never lowers prices. It responds to slack demand by putting fewer diamonds in the sightholders' boxes, creating an artificial scarcity to prop up prices. Sometimes BeBeers forces the diamond producers to sit on a portion of their rough, while still forbidding outside sales.

Chronic unprofitability of diamond cutters has recently caused DeBeers to change the assortments in the sight boxes to a more profitable mix. The cost of cutting accounts for a mere 2% of the retail price of diamonds.

DeBeers argues that it stabilizes diamond prices by releasing or withholding from its stockpile, provides the huge amounts of capital to develop new mines and spends millions on advertising to promote the mystique and value of diamonds to consumers. The slogan "A diamond is forever", which sounds like an ancient folk proverb, was actually coined by the N.W. Ayer advertising agency in 1948 for DeBeers. This is arguably the most successful advertising campaign in history.

The Japanese had no diamond engagement ring tradition until a DeBeers campaign after the war. Now 70% of Japanese brides wear a diamond. DeBeers spent $180 million in 2001 on consumer advertising and plans a like amount for 2002.

But there have been strains in the "single channel marketing" system. In 1996, the huge Argyle mine in Australia declined to renew its contract to sell most of its production to DeBeers. Argyle produces mostly small, low quality diamonds, which are cut in low-wage India for mass-market jewelry. DeBeers had lowered the price it would pay for these diamonds as a blow to the Russians, who were leaking quantities of these diamonds outside the system.

With DeBeers' market share having slipped from 85% to 57% and its inventory swollen to $4.5 billion it undertook an historic reorganization.

In 2000, DeBeers said it would no longer try to control the world diamond supply. The company went private in June 2001, being bought by three companies in which it had partial or complete ownership. It initiated a program in which its sightholders will be required to develop marketing and branding programs and will be judged accordingly. This has instilled great fear in DeBeers' sightholders. This "Supplier of Choice" program was voluntarily submitted to the European Commission for review of anticompetitiveness. The Commission issued some objections and the program was on hold for a few years but was approved in 2003.

In the meantime, DeBeers has sweetened the pot by giving the sightholders a more profitable assortment of rough diamonds in their boxes. Diamond prices have actually declined slightly in the last couple of years, the first time I have seen this.

DeBeers also is entering the retail market. They have partnered with LVMH (Louis Vuitton Moet Hennessy), the European luxury goods retailer to sell diamonds with a DeBeers brand in their stores. This required a mandatory submission to the European Commission, and was approved. The first store opened in a posh London neighborhood in November, 2002. But the shelves were mostly bare. It seems they didn't get the merchandise in time. Even I know how to do that. A second store will open near Tiffany in New York in 2004.

The fear is that DeBeers will allocate the best diamonds at the best prices to this venture, to the detriment of the rest of the diamond world. It looks like Tiffany isn't waiting to find out: they've arranged to buy diamonds straight from Canadian mines. At any rate, it's very upscale and shouldn't apply to most of you.

In my own experience, way down the food chain from such giants as DeBeers, wholesalers always covet the greater profits of retailers, while ignoring the one-at-a-time quantities of retail, with its excruciating customer service, for which wholesalers are temperamentally unsuited, which is why they became wholesalers, and not retailers.

14. The Rap Sheet

When you are shopping for a diamond, you will see jewelers consulting a red price list. This is the Rapaport Diamond Report and it is the price bible. (There are other price lists, but no one I know uses them.) Diamonds are listed by shape and by color and clarity within carat weight ranges. It is published once a week for round diamonds, once a month for pear shape diamonds. The other fancy shapes are keyed via different discounts to the pear shape list.

The prices listed in the Rap sheet are not the real wholesale prices. The real prices are discounts from the sheet. The discount percentage for a given carat weight, color, and clarity is determined by the quality of the cut and whether the diamond falls in the upper or lower end of the weight range. For example, in the 1.00 to 1.49 carat range, 1.25 to 1.49 carat diamonds will cost 5-10% more per carat than 1.00 to 1.24 carat diamonds. It's the magic size effect. A .99 carat diamond costs less than a 1.00 carat diamond, and is in a different price grouping, even though it could be the same size or slightly larger than the 1 carat diamond.

The sheet specifically states "Very Fine Ideal and Excellent Cuts in 0.30 and larger sizes bring 10% to 20% premiums over normal cuts." The sheet is based on average-good cuts, allowing tables of up to 64% and total depths down to 57.5%. Lousy cuts have a steep discount. An ideal cut can cost 25-30% more than a deficient cut. That's a lot of money in diamonds costing thousands of dollars and it cautions against the common consumer practice of shopping diamonds only on color and clarity.

One sales ploy is to sell a diamond "at the sheet." The customer is shown the price of a diamond on the sheet and is told that he or she is getting the diamond at wholesale. Actually, most diamonds can be sold "at the sheet" and yield a standard profit since diamonds are sold wholesale with discounts from the sheet. FTC regulations forbid advertising "wholesale to the public" unless the diamond, or other merchandise, is sold at cost.

The Rapaport Diamond Report was first published 25 years ago, to great consternation and hostility in the diamond trade. It was felt at that time that it was a step toward the commoditization of a product that had been traditionally sold on its mystique and romance. Well, mystique and romance are fine to a point, but with diamonds now costing thousands of dollars due to the relentless price increases of DeBeers, that point has been passed. Price is important. But you already know that.

15. The Fifth C – Cost

An ad in the Nov. 22, 1943 issue of Life Magazine lists a range of prices for diamonds: ½ carat, $200-350; 1 carat, $400-800; 2 carats, $1050-2500. You wish! But how big was the paycheck?

Diamonds are very expensive, so expensive that in order to sell them at all, competition has lowered profits of diamond cutters, wholesalers, and retailers to a minimum. In a major metropolitan area you should easily be able to buy a ¾ carat or larger diamond carrying a profit of from 15-25%. If you encounter wildly different prices for similar diamonds, it will be the result of misgrading or differences in the cut (Fifth Avenue/Rodeo Drive stores excluded).

My store is in the New York metropolitan area and there are at least 10 jewelry stores within a 5 mile radius of me. In addition, I have to compete with mall jewelry stores, department stores, so-called jewelry exchanges, and 47th Street, the New York diamond district, about an hour away and a short trip when thousands of dollars are at stake.

Profits at the wholesaler level are so slim that there is very little difference between what the big store and the small store pays. Real volume buying is far beyond the means of single stores or small chains, requiring frequent trips to, or a permanent buying office in, Belgium, India, or Israel, the major diamond cutting centers. You would think that national chain stores would pay bottom dollar from wholesalers, but it ain't necessarily so. These types of stores demand long payment terms and extensive return privileges from suppliers.

People hear or read ads for diamond jewelry and the prices in these ads, even though they are for junk, stick in their minds as the going rate. Tennis bracelets seem to be especially vulnerable to this cheaper than thou syndrome. I often get customers coming to buy a tennis bracelet with a budget about half of reality. They're shocked at the incredible disparity in price between what they expect to pay and the cost of what is, in fact, reasonably priced quality jewelry.

Diamonds that were once crushed into industrial abrasive are now cut into gems and some consumers, inculcated with both the diamond mystique and the American bargain mystique, will buy them, even though their lack of brilliance is obvious to anyone with eyes to see. I once had a diamond dealer come to the store and offer a 1 carat diamond for $150 wholesale. "This I have to see," I thought to myself. The diamond was white, even reasonably well-cut. Not that it mattered. It was so full of cracks, with a few chunks out, that it looked like pieces of crushed glass glued together.

Forget the sale prices in ads you see. With few exceptions, you can be sure the original price was calibrated just to run the sale. The "retail comparison prices" shown by catalog and TV retailers fall into this category. Funny how they're always able to trounce the "retail" price. There's always smoke from this house. One day it's going to burn.

Other than for watches, there is no list price or "manufacturer's suggested retail price" for jewelry. Therefore there is nothing to discount from. In other words, they're making it up. You *can* fool some of the people all of the time.

Quality jewelry is not advertised on the basis of price. Discount merchandising inevitably leads to selling cheap stuff cheap, not good stuff cheap, since it attracts the type of customer who only wants to hear price. And it repels customers who hear "discount" or "affordable" or "70% off" as the other kind of cheap. This forces such a store to cut corners on quality to satisfy its self-selected clientele. It's so predictable that I can tell my customers from what type of retailer – department store, jewelry exchange, or TV – their jewelry was bought by the type of corner-cutting I see.

"How much do you want to spend?" This is the classic opening line to a bad sales pitch. Actually, it strikes to the heart of the matter, since diamonds can get seriously expensive. What size diamond do you want really means how much can you afford. Set a budget. Then add 20%. Nobody ever said the diamond they bought cost less than they expected. And don't forget about the sales tax. (See p. 94.)

Don't be coy about revealing your budget, in due course, to the salesperson. It saves time for both parties. If you can't afford an excellent large diamond, buy an excellent smaller one, or wait until you've saved more. A good deal on a bad diamond is no bargain.

Sometimes you really can get it wholesale. For a variety of reasons, people sell their diamonds to jewelry stores. They're bought for a lot less than wholesale. If they're badly cut or old mine diamonds that are bought to be recut, the price paid is very low. Nobody ever went broke taking a profit, so these diamonds are often sold at about wholesale, especially around rent time at the end of the month. But it's hit-or-miss to find what you want when you want it. This also speaks to the notion of buying a diamond as an investment. If you bid at auction for important jewelry, where there is no wholesale or retail, you might make out. Otherwise, you will find that you buy retail and sell below wholesale.

Finally, most diamonds I've seen that were bought from a friend or relative in the business were not so hot. I have no advice on how you can handle this problem.

16. Shopping — The Right Things in the Right Places

Guess who sells the most jewelry. Tiffany, Cartier, Harry Winston? Wrong. It's Wal-Mart. Tiffany is #8, behind Zales, Sterling, J.C. Penney, Sears, Finlay (operates department store jewelry departments), and QVC. This should tell you something.

Famous name stores that sell fine clothing, gifts, or kitchenware do not necessarily also sell fine diamonds. The largest jeweler in your area is not necessarily the best. Stores geared to the mass market sell diamonds suitable for the mass market. Trust me, you don't want a mass-market diamond.

Beware of gimmicks and general claims of wonderfulness. If everyone sells fine diamonds, then where are all those crummy diamonds I see coming from? And price hounds beware: you can easily avoid wounding your ego by shooting yourself in the foot.

You don't necessarily have to go to a luxe store, either. My store is an ordinary jewelry store in a middle class town. But I only sell fine diamonds. Don't confuse posh display with superior product or assume that utilitarian decor showcases mediocrity. Excellence results from people being committed to excellence for its own sake, in a variety of styles.

These industrial diamonds in a wedding band are typical of mass-market jewelry.

Fig. 61

You should first look for a knowledgeable person behind the counter who takes pride in the diamonds he or she sells. It is much more difficult to sell a poor diamond when one knows it's poor. Most jewelers are bad liars, just like you.

Superficial knowledge, however, makes it easy to rationalize that a diamond is "decent." The salesperson may only have experience with what the store sells, and have never seen fine quality diamonds, or may be unaware of, or unable to evaluate, the nuances of cut so important to the appearance of a diamond.

One customer showed me the marquise diamond he had bought with the assurance from the seller that it was the finest diamond he had ever sold. I'd hate to see his usual fare: the diamond was an I1 clarity. Another customer bought a diamond cluster ring because she had been told that the jeweler had originally made it for his wife. The ring was okay, but not jeweler's-wife quality. (You should see the diamond heart I made for my wife.) I presume sincerity but ignorance on the part of these sellers. So does one cross the line from positive spin to unwitting misrepresentation. Salespeople need to take pride in what they do, just like you.

You should be offered a look through a microscope at larger diamonds, especially engagement ring stones. But remember, diamonds are graded at 10 power, and at higher magnifications you may think that inclusions are worse than they are. But the salesperson should allow you to see the diamonds at any magnification. A jewelers loupe is not a substitute for for a binocular gemological microscope with darkfield illumination (lighting through the sides of the stone that makes inclusions stand out). Using a loupe on a diamond is the macho thing to do in the diamond world, but I've never been able to see much through the damn thing. If a store doesn't have a microscope, it is unprofessional.

The salesperson should be a gemologist[14], or at least have taken both the GIA diamonds and diamond grading courses (the diamonds component of the gemologist program). Some salespeople take only the diamonds course and not the hands-on diamond grading course, or take a one-week introductory course at the GIA.

An engagement ring diamond should generally be bought loose, then mounted. Don't fall in love with a ring and wind up with whatever diamond is in it. Put your money into the cut first, color second, and clarity third. However, color and clarity should be reasonably good. A well cut diamond will be marred by eye-visible flaws. Although it is an article of faith that a white diamond is better, you don't have to agree. You may even prefer a yellowish diamond, although I've never had a customer who did.

You may have difficulty finding a well cut diamond in the lower color and clarity grades. The discriminating stores and consumers willing to pay more for fine cutting also demand higher quality all

14. A gemologist has been awarded that title by the Gemological Institute of America, or equivalent foreign institution. Gemologists (or jewelry appraisers), unlike hairdressers, are not licensed or certified by any governmental board or body. So there is no such thing as a "licensed" or "certified" gemologist (or appraiser, except for real estate). There is, however, a "certified gemologist" and "certified gemologist appraiser" title awarded by the American Gem Society.

A gemologist diploma can be earned by a six month residence course at the GIA in New York or Carlsbad, California, or by home study, which takes several years, with the mailing of specimens back and forth. The residence course confers the title "Graduate Gemologist" (G.G.); a home study graduate is titled "Gemologist." Home study gemologists can earn the Graduate Gemologist title by taking three one-week residence courses.

around. Lower color and clarity diamonds are more likely to be cut to maximize weight.

This process does not necessarily work in reverse. There are plenty of high color and clarity diamonds that are poorly cut. People want their kids to be geniuses and their diamonds to be white and flawless. Since awareness of cut, which is not so neatly categorized as clarity and color, is dim to nonexistent to the public and many jewelry salespeople alike, diamonds that are clean and white but don't shine as they should are very salable.

Feel free to buy a diamond at one store and the setting at another. It would be foolish to pass up a diamond you like because you don't see the setting you want. You won't hurt anyone's feelings by giving half a sale rather than no sale.

Allow plenty of time to shop for an engagement ring. A man running out just before Christmas or Valentine's Day to buy an engagement ring is at great risk for diamond disappointment. Many stores have a stock of engagement ring settings and a few loose diamonds. Often, diamonds or ring mountings have to be ordered in for you to see. The jeweler gets diamonds "on memo", borrows them to show you and returns them if there's no sale. Diamonds are usually obtained in a few days. Settings can take a couple of weeks. All this takes time. Allow for it.

Also, don't think you can always walk in and get the size and quality of diamond you want immediately. During one of DeBeer's periodic cutbacks and around the holidays, popular sizes and qualities dry up and it can take quite a search to find them.

The above is doubly true for ideal cuts. There just aren't that many of them out there. And when you need a certain size, color, and clarity also, it narrows the field to just a few for each wholesaler.

You can save money by buying a diamond just under a "magic size" – 1/2, 3/4, 1 carat, etc. A .95 carat diamond will cost less per carat than a full carat, and the difference in size will be small.

Put your money into the diamond first and the ring setting second. It would be foolish to sacrifice the quality of the diamond to be able to afford an expensive setting. Better to have a gorgeous diamond in an inexpensive plain ring than a mediocre diamond in a striking setting. You can always have the diamond remounted in the future.

And speaking of engagement ring settings, try to avoid the dutiful man syndrome. In this syndrome, the woman points out a ring in a store, on another woman, or in an ad picture, and proclaims that that's the ring she wants. The man then dutifully sets out to find that exact ring, usually without success. It's a big jewelry universe out there, with thousands of manufacturers and millions of styles. I get about half a trash bag a week of catalogs in the mail. Usually, the man can find something similar, but not exact. The ornamentally challenged male being common, the poor guy persists in his quest for the holy sale. But usually, the woman isn't *that* finicky and close will work. If you fall into this category, try discussing similar versus exact at the moment of revelation.

I had one guy come in with a picture off the internet of a plain tiffany setting (a tiffany setting is just the prongs on top and a thin gold band on the bottom), but with a wider and flatter than usual shank (the band part of the ring). Of course, I couldn't turn it up in any of my catalogs. The guy went back for indirect consultations, planning to casually bring up the topic when opportune, since the ring was planned to be a surprise. But the difference between his ring and a standard tiffany is very minor, and would in any case be overshadowed by the diamond, since a tiffany setting is designed to be a minimal, simple ring.

It may be a little premature, but when buying an engagement ring, you should also plan the wedding. Make sure an engagement ring setting is compatible with a wedding band if they are going to be worn together on the same finger. Buy a setting that will fit next to a straight-edged band, that is one half of an interlocking set (and be sure the other half will be available when needed), or one that will work with a wrap or insert.

A wrap is a ring that is designed to fit next to a plain tiffany setting. It usually has a grouping of small diamonds or trillions on the sides with a small metal bridge between. The sides of the wrap fit over the shoulders of the tiffany and the bridge fits under the head holding the diamond, giving the appearance of a diamond with side stones. An insert is also designed for a tiffany ring. An insert is two rings, usually V-shaped and with small diamonds, soldered together back-to-back with spacers between them to create a slot for the engagement ring to slide into. The shank of the engagement ring is hidden inside the slot and the diamond sticks out above. The effect is of a single, wider ring.

The prongs of a tiffany setting stick out at the base where the head is soldered into the narrower ring shank. This means a regular straight-edged wedding band will not fit flush against the engagement ring. Special thin gold bands are available for tiffanies that have a notch in them at the top to fit the protruding prong. Such a band should be ordered from the same manufacturer as the tiffany. This will ensure a perfect fit since, although tiffanies are pretty standard, there will be slight differences from one manufacturer to another. Actually, you might as well order the band at the same time as the engagement ring, as these bands are inexpensive.

If you buy an engagement ring that is incompatible with a straight-edge band, you may have to have a wedding band custommade to fit. This is done by carving the fitting ring in wax and then having the ring cast by the lost-wax method. When I do this, I usually heat the engagement ring slightly with a torch (it won't hurt the ring or the diamond), and quickly press a wax tube section against it. The wax melts into one side of the engagement ring, giving a perfect auto-fit. The wax is then filed to shape from the other side. This is naturally labor-intensive and more expensive than an off-the-shelf ring. And it's not done while you wait: you will have to leave your engagement ring for a few days.

Rings that curve or bulge are likely candidates for wedding band problems. The simplest way to see if a regular wedding band will fit is to try it. The jeweler should have plenty of wedding bands on hand. For engagement rings with heads that curve out slightly, there are catalog bands with a curved top section that may work; they are designed for this purpose.

An anniversary band, a ring with diamonds set all around, or an engagement ring with diamonds around the bottom of the shank, can only be sized with difficulty, by cutting out or adding a diamond. Some types of these rings can't be sized. Also, diamonds on the bottom of your finger are more likely to get chipped when you grip something or slap your hand down.

In engagement rings, the head, the cage with prongs that holds the diamond is almost always made of white metal. The idea is that since you've paid for the non-yellowness of your diamond, it wouldn't do to surround it with yellow gold. (In fact, most diamond heads are unavailable in yellow gold.) Most diamond heads today are 14 karat white gold. White gold is usually made by the addition of nickel to gold. Nickel white gold is susceptible to stress corrosion cracking, whereby chemicals, especially chlorine, attack the boundaries between the microscopic grains of the alloy. This is most pronounced where the metal is stressed, such as where the prongs are folded over the diamond. This can lead to a sudden shearing off of a prong. This process happens invisibly and is cumulative: prongs can suddenly crack with no immediate cause. I had one customer who decided to clean her jewelry in chlorine bleach. All the yellow and white gold turned black and all the prongs cracked off her engagement ring. Fortunately, she didn't lose her fine, expensive 1½ carat diamond.

Now that I've scared you to death, let me say that most people go through life without incident. It happens only occasionally. But if it does happen, you could lose your diamond. You should avoid contact with chlorine products, such as bleach, sink cleanser, photographic chemicals, and even swimming pool water.

There is another type of white gold: palladium white gold. Palladium is a white metal in the platinum family. Palladium white gold does not suffer from stress corrosion cracking. But it's hard to find. No doubt this is because palladium is much more expensive than the nickel it would replace. I can only get it in a few types of heads from one company.

The premier metal for setting diamonds is platinum. This metal is invulnerable to everything except mercury and is stronger than white gold. It's soft and will scratch like gold, but it has much better resistance to wear because it is so dense, 70% heavier than 14 karat gold. This is immediately noticeable when filing, sawing, or polishing platinum – it's work! Platinum jewelry is about 3½ times more expensive than 14 karat gold jewelry. One reason for this is that platinum is so much heavier – the same piece of jewelry in platinum weighs much more than 14 karat gold, and precious metals are sold by weight. Another reason is that platinum jewelry is more pure than 14 or 18 karat gold[15]. 14 karat gold is 58.3% gold and 18 karat is 75% gold. But platinum jewelry is 90 or 95% platinum. And platinum is much more expensive than gold. But a 1 carat size platinum head will only add about $50 to the cost of a ring.

Four prongs or six? Engagement rings in which the diamond is set high above the ring itself, which is most engagement rings, should have six prong heads. With four prongs, if one prong tip cracks off or is worn down with time, the diamond will likely be lost. With six prongs, it will not. With six prong heads, the prongs are a little lighter than four prong heads and one or two are occasionally bent sideways in the course of everyday activity, but the worst that will happen is that the diamond will become loose, but not lost. Bent prongs and loose diamonds are easily fixed by a jeweler.

Certain types of rings in which the diamond is set low will have four prongs. This is much less dangerous. The prongs are usually stubby and heavy and there is much less leverage to bend a prong back should it get caught and pulled than with the long, high prongs of the usual engagement ring.

---

15. The karat number of gold refers to how many parts in 24 are gold. Pure gold is 24 karat. 14 karat gold is 14/24ths, or 58.3% gold. To figure the percentage of gold for any karat, just divide the karat number by 24.

It is not true that diamonds that are set down in the metal of a mounting will show less brilliance than diamonds set such that the pavilion is exposed. Diamonds are designed to reflect light that enters from the top, not from the bottom.

Be wary of rings in which small diamonds are set between bars of gold. If the ring bends, the bars will pull away from some of the diamonds and they will fall out. Bar settings should be heavy, top and bottom, to prevent bending. However, with tennis bracelets, the bars are decorative, the diamonds being secured with prongs.

Make sure diamond stud earrings match. You'd be surprised how different table sizes can make two diamonds the same size look mismatched. Also, make sure friction backs grip the post securely. Many earrings come with light-weight backs. Heavy backs only cost $10 a pair, a good investment for expensive diamond earrings. Screw backs, which screw on to a threaded post can work loose and the post can feel thick and uncomfortable in the ear. There's also a push-on screw-off type in which the post is threaded but the back is not. The metal around the hole in the back is flanged such that it works with the thread on the post. Avoid them. The backs are too thin and bend easily.

There's a new type of locking back with a spring-loaded disc that locks into slots in a special post. The disc has tabs that are squeezed to unlock it. But keep the disc clean. Ear stuff can jam the mechanism in the open position and the disc can slip off.

Some diamonds come with a logo and serial numbers laser-inscribed on the girdle for identification. This is an excellent security feature. You can also have a personal message inscribed.

Laser inscriptions

Photo courtesy of Sirius
Diamonds Ltd.

Fig. 62

17. The Appraisal Mess

Incompetent and wildly inflated appraisals are the bane of the jewelry industry.

Just being a jeweler does not qualify one to do appraisals. To be a qualified appraiser, one must first be a gemologist. Since there is nothing in the gemology training about what jewelry costs or retail prices or how to value jewelry for appraisals, one must also have appraisal training.

There are different types of appraisals – divorce, estate, liquidation, barter, donation, and insurance replacement. And these different types of appraisals would set different values on the same piece of jewelry. All except insurance replacement require advanced appraisal training and are outside the scope of regular jewelry store practice. But most appraisals are for insurance purposes, and that is the type of appraisal most jewelers do.

An appraisal is an expert opinion of the quality and market value of jewelry for the purpose of obtaining insurance. And so, *the insurance replacement price* given in the appraisal should be the real market price of the jewelry in the usual type of store in which it is sold and in the area in which the insured lives.

It is widely believed that unless an appraisal values jewelry for more than was paid, the customer paid too much. Here's a poser for you. The goal of an appraisal is to state the market price to replace a lost diamond. Most things most of the time the time sell at the market price, because what most things sell for most of the time *is* the market price. If everybody's diamond appraises for 50% more than was paid, how much above average should the average diamond cost? Get the picture? The insurance companies aren't fooled. They collect excess premiums based on inflated appraisals but pay out the true cost for a loss.

There are two methods of valuation: the market data method and the cost method.

The market data method entails getting prices from different stores in the client's area which ordinarily sell the type of jewelry being appraised and using the most commonly occurring price, not the average price, which is called the mode.

The cost method is to determine what the item would cost the jeweler and apply the jeweler's usual markup for that type of jewelry to arrive at a replacement price. The jewelry is thus valued at what is, or would be, the actual selling price in the appraiser's store. Since the jewelry business is intensely competitive, especially for diamonds, the usual items brought in for appraisal, the appraiser's store is considered representative of other stores in the area.

The market data method is not suitable for jewelers, since they can hardly call up their competitors and ask them what they sell their jewelry for. Independent appraisers say that the market data method is the only one that reflects the market, by sampling actual transaction prices, and is the only valid one. May be, but my phone book has no listings for independent jewelry appraisers.

To make a living at appraising jewelry, an appraiser has to be located in a wealthy area and get the big, expensive pieces and the important estate jewelry. This leaves the jewelry stores to do the appraising for the rest and most of us. The GIA has recognized that jewelry stores are going to be doing most of the appraisals anyway, and so instituted a home-study appraisal course in 1999. Conventional appraisal training is difficult to get for someone tied to retail store hours, and in any case is based on the market data method.

Jewelers feel forced to give appraisals, whether they are qualified or not, for fear of looking unprofessional. The public believes that jewelers do appraisals and that jewelers who don't do appraisals aren't real jewelers. I doubt that the average consumer is even aware that there is such a thing as an independent jewelry appraiser. Jewelers also feel forced to give appraisals on the diamonds they sell for fear of getting low-balled: a deliberate understatement of value by a another jeweler trying to make himself look better than the competition. Consumers, ever fearful of a rip-off, are inclined to believe the lower price, rather than question the competence of the appraiser. And besides, it's not good business to send a customer to see what another store has.

The cost method works well for jewelry within the normal range of goods sold by the appraising store. Outside that range it's not so easy to determine cost. Suppliers are not necessarily forthcoming with non-customers and non-potential-customers. For very expensive pieces the jeweler doesn't sell and is unfamiliar with, an incorrect appraisal value can have serious consequences. Too low an appraisal and the client would not receive enough from insurance to cover a loss. Too high and the client would pay excess premiums, and premiums on expensive jewelry are also expensive. When large sums are involved, these cases usually wind up in court and the appraiser usually loses.

Also, an appraiser must be familiar with the hallmarks of name designers and stores. The appraised value of this jewelry is what it is sold for in these types of stores, not that of equivalent but generic jewelry. The appraiser must know this and must be able to find out this information. This is best left to either independent appraisers or very upscale jewelers who are familiar with this type of jewelry.

Appraisals for antique or estate jewelry should only be done by jewelers familiar with the market for these types of pieces. This type of jewelry cannot be valued by adding up the costs of the components to make a new piece. They are old pieces and part of the valuation is their age. They have a market different from new jewelry. I do not do appraisals of antique jewelry.

Appraisals for items sold by the appraising store should value the jewelry at the price for which it was sold to the client and say so in the appraisal, unless an explanation, such as a one-time price reduction, is clearly stated. It is unethical, and perhaps illegal, to say that something is worth more than you sold it for without substantiation. Inflated appraisal prices often are due to a jeweler without appraisal training assuming that there is some mythical "retail" price out there. Of course, he's always cheaper than the "retail".

I had a customer show me both the bill of sale and the appraisal given by the seller for a diamond he had bought a few years ago. The selling price was $2450 and the appraisal was for $3500. This is flat-out unethical and the seller, a by appointment office-type operation, should have known it. And the kicker is that I could have sold that diamond for $2000 without breaking a sweat and would have given an appraisal value in that amount.

Here's a cautionary tale at the low end that appeared in a trade magazine and illustrates the pitfalls of appraising without knowledge of appraisal valuation.

A major discount store chain was selling a gemstone and diamond necklace. The department manager took one of them incognito to a local jeweler for an appraisal. The jeweler analyzed what the components would cost him and his labor to make the piece. The result was the discount store advertising that the jewelry appraised for double its price. The item was a mass-produced piece made with cheap labor in Asia and sold at a quantity price. A custom-made duplicate is not comparable. You could hand-make a light bulb, but it's still worth what light bulbs sell for.

I see this type of cheap gemstone and diamond jewelry brought in for repairs all the time. Fortunately, it's inexpensive enough that people don't need appraisals for it. I don't have a clue what it sells for, since I don't sell it. And I wouldn't know where to find it or how to find out what it would cost me. The suppliers of this type of merchandise live in their own world, accessible only to large chain-store purchasers. Coincidently in light of the story above, I had worked out a rule of thumb when importuned by customers for verbal appraisals of this type of jewelry: figure out what it would cost me to make it by assembling the components and what I would sell it for, then divide by two. This method gets close to the prices people tell me they paid.

An appraisal should state that the appraiser is competent to appraise the item, list his or her qualifications, and be signed. Any interest the appraiser has in the item being appraised, i.e. If the jewelry was sold by the appraiser's store, should be clearly stated. In such a case, the selling price should be disclosed and if the insurance replacement price is different from the selling price, the reason for this should be stated.

An appraisal should have an extensive, detailed description of the jewelry, with measurements and grades of diamonds or other gemstones, and a plot of larger diamonds. Due diligence requires that colored stones be positively identified with gemological instruments, usually by measuring the refractive index and determining its crystal type with a polariscope. (See appendix on gemology.) Hand-written appraisals or off-the-shelf appraisal forms are unprofessional.

Sometimes jewelry will appraise for a lot more than it was sold for due to the methodology inherent in setting an insurance replacement price.

Certain types of retail operations only sell closeouts or special purchase items. Of course, they're cheap. They wouldn't have bought them unless they could sell them cheap, because that's what they do. But once it's gone, that's it. You can't call them up and order a new piece if you lose the one you bought from them. This is a "what we have when we have it" price.

But an insurance replacement price is what you would have to pay to replace a lost item at any time. This is a "what you want when you want it" price. Keep this in mind when told by such an outlet that the jewelry they're selling will appraise for much more.

I suspect that many bad appraisals come from the reluctance of consumers to leave their diamonds. Doing a proper appraisal takes time: measuring, grading clarity and color, and taking notes. Sometimes it can take over an hour just to get a stubbornly dirty diamond ring microscope-clean. This is not a while-you-wait process for most stores.

But many people don't want to let their diamond out of their sight. And so they have it appraised by the first store that will do it in front of them, whether the appraiser is competent or not. In larger stores, with a gemologist on staff, it can be done while you wait, usually by appointment. But in many small stores, the proprietor is the staff, and he or she has to do everything else, too. Retail routine consists of constant small interruptions: the phone rings, a salesman comes in, changing a watch battery, taking in repairs, schmoozing with customers, and, once in a while, selling something.

Even though I have a procedure for putting people's minds at ease, by letting them see their diamond through the microscope and showing them a distinctive inclusion or natural, I don't even bring it up with very suspicious people, in hopes that they'll leave.

I once had a woman come into the store for (a free) evaluation of an earring with two small channel set diamonds. She never took her eyes off me and followed me in lockstep whenever I moved. She repeated to me the maxim of never letting your diamond out of your sight. When I put her earring under the microscope, the diamonds looked like they were coated with bacon grease. When I asked her indulgence to go in the back room for a few seconds to steam the earring, she took it back and retreated out of the store.

A jeweler friend of mine agreed to repair an engagement ring while the customer watched. His store, unlike mine, has the workbench in the back of the showroom. When he swiveled in his chair to get a tool, momentarily turning his back to the customer, the customer demanded to know what he was doing. He turned back, gave the ring to the customer, and bade him farewell.

A newly engaged young girl came in with her mother for an appraisal of her ring in the afternoon. She was leaving the next day and I agreed to have the appraisal ready by the next morning. I began right away and, with the usual interruptions, had my notes ready to type within a few hours. I even took a through-the-microscope picture of her diamond to put on the appraisal, since the inclusions showed up well and this would be quicker and better than a plot of the diamond. Then the girl came back, sans mère. Her fiancé had instructed her to wait in the store until the appraisal was completed or get the ring back. She got the ring back. But I had the last laugh. A picture of her diamond is fig. 10 on page 21.

The following examples will show you what is involved in an appraisal. I have omitted my store letterhead from the cover page and generalized it for purposes of illustration. I include this cover page in all appraisals.

The inclusions in the plot are actually in red. The replacement price plus sales tax would follow the description.

Insurance Replacement Appraisal

Attached is an insurance replacement appraisal for:

Name
Address
Phone

I have no interest in the subject of this report and no bias with respect to the party involved.

Neither my compensation nor the consummation of any sale is contingent upon the reporting of any predetermined replacement price.

I am competent to identify and appraise the merchandise described in this report; it is within the range of goods normally bought and sold by (Store name). All significant characteristics affecting the replacement price have been reported.

I have personally inspected the property described in this report and I have graded the gemstones as accurately as possible by accepted gemological methods and standards. However, opinions of quality and grade are subjective and may vary upon examination by another qualified grader. This appraisal is therefore an expert opinion and is not to be construed as a warranty.

Appraiser signature
Title
Qualifications

The line "I have no interest in the subject of this report and no bias with respect to the party involved." is replaced with the following for an appraisal of jewelry sold by the store.

"This Appraisal is provided at no charge by (store name) as a customer service. The jewelry described in this appraisal was sold by (store name). The sale was not contingent upon providing this appraisal, nor on any predetermined replacement price."

Marquise Diamond Engagement Ring

The ring features a center marquise diamond with 2 diamond tapered baguettes on either side of the center. The baguettes measure 5.75 x 2.25 x 1.25mm and are VVS in clarity and G-H in color with an estimated total weight of .42 carat. The center is set in a 6 prong die-struck platinum tulip head and the baguettes are set in platinum boxes. The ring shank is an 18 karat yellow gold casting and is stamped "10 IRID PLAT HEAD" and "18K PSP". Sizing balls are soldered inside the ring shank. The ring weighs 4.7 grams in total. Measurements and color and clarity grading are subject to the limitation of the mounting. The details of the center diamond are as follows.

Estimated Weight: 1.22 carat

Color: H - I

Clarity: SI1

Measurements: 10.1 x 5.75 mm

Estimated Total depth: 3.62mm, 63%

Table: 3.25mm , 56.5%

Girdle: slightly thick, faceted

Culet: none

Fluorescence: Strong blue

Comment: grain lines not plotted

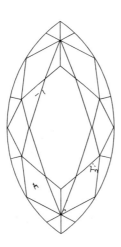

Fig. 63

Key to symbols

⌐ ⌐ ∖ ↑ Feather

92

Diamond Pendant

The pendant consists of a 2.45 carat round brilliant diamond burnish-set in a 14 karat yellow gold cast bezel. The pendant weighs 4.4 grams in total. The diamond was recut from 2.63 carats by (My Store) to remove chips. The pendant mounting was sold by (My Store) for $xxx including labor. The replacement price for the pendant mounting is the same. The details of the diamond are as follows.

Weight: 2.45 carat

Color: G

Clarity: SI1

Measurements: 8.68x8.74x5.26mm

Depth: 60.4%

Table: 5.32mm, 61.1%

Girdle: thin-med, faceted

Culet: none

Fluorescence: none

Fig. 64

18. Recutting Your Diamond

If your diamond is chipped or you are unhappy with its appearance, you should consider having it recut. You will lose a little size and a little weight. How much depends on how deep the chip or how badly proportioned the diamond. Old mine and old European cuts will lose 20-35% of their weight. The reduction in diameter will depend on how out of round the diamond is, how shallow the pavilion, and how large the culet. A squarish old mine cut will have to be rounded by cutting down to the least dimension. A diamond with too shallow a pavilion, which is common in these stones, will have to be reduced in diameter until the minimal angle to avoid a fish-eye can be reached. To close up the large culets on these diamonds can take a lot off the size. The culet can still be left somewhat large by modern standards to save weight.

The diamond in the appraisal example on the preceding page was recut to remove several small chips. It also improved in brilliance. The recutting pushed this diamond under the 2.50 carat magic size and reduced its value. But the customer was more concerned with appearance than value. She didn't want to sell the diamond, she wanted to wear it. And at any rate it's still a big diamond.

I had one diamond recut to get out a small chip and it lost no weight at all! This diamond weighed .56 carat before and after. Diamonds are weighed to 1/100th of a carat (1 point). It must have weighed .564 carat before and .556 carat after, and the electronic scale rounded off both weights to the same figure.

Recutting is at your risk. It is very rare, but occasionally diamonds shatter on the wheel for no reason. It has never happened to me or to my diamond cutter (on a recut), but it is possible. The diamond is checked for internal strain, which shows under polarized light, before cutting. Don't forget, your diamond already passed the stress test when it was originally cut. If you are considering having your diamond recut, make sure your jeweler states beforehand who is assuming the risk.

I've only had one customer decline to have a diamond recut because of the risk. Of course, if a diamond is badly chipped you will have to have it recut regardless. In a way, this makes the decision easier since the diamond is no good to you as is and its value would in any case be as recut.

The cost is $200-300 per carat, with the 1 carat price as the minimum. Recut weight can usually be estimated by a gemologist.

19. Maintenance — Wear and Tear and Care

The mission of a diamond is to shine. Dirty diamonds don't shine. Most diamonds are never really clean, even if you think they're clean.

Diamond has a chemical affinity for grease and oil, so much so that diamonds are separated from crushed ore by vibrating the ore over a grease table. The diamonds stick to the grease and the gravel falls away.

In the course of everyday living, your diamonds will quickly become coated with oily dirt, soap residue, powder, etc. The optical properties that enable a diamond to shine, high refraction and small critical angle, operate at the boundary between two substances. Your diamond shines because this boundary is between diamond and air.

Diamond's refractive index of 2.417 is defined relative to air which has a refractive index of 1. Grease has a refractive index of about 1.5. If your diamond becomes coated with greasy dirt on the bottom, its relative refractive index will be reduced by 2.417/1.5, to about that of topaz. And the critical angle, the window for light to escape, will be over 50% larger at the diamond/grease boundary than the critical angle at the diamond/air boundary. Much more light will leak out the bottom of the diamond rather than be reflected out the top and the diamond will lose brilliance. This is why flaws that are otherwise masked by by the brilliance of a diamond become visible when the diamond is dirty.

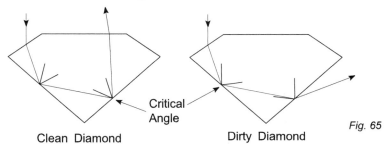

Clean Diamond   Dirty Diamond

Critical Angle

Fig. 65

A thick coating of dirt on the bottom of a diamond, stuck inaccessibly underneath prongs and seats is very tenacious and can be difficult to get off. This is why gemstone jewelry has openings underneath stones – for cleaning.

For appraisals or before attempting repairs that involve soldering near a diamond, it must be surgically clean. Dirt underneath diamonds that is fried by soldering will reflect around the stone and make it look dark and it is even more difficult to remove. I've had hidden greasy dirt underneath diamonds actually ignite and burn with a flame when soldering. Sometimes heating the diamond even more to completely carbonize the dirt works. Sometimes the only way to get it out is to boil the jewelry in lye.

So when I clean a diamond, I inspect it under a microscope to be sure all the dirt is gone. I am amazed at how long this can take. I've put jewelry in my professional ultrasonic cleaner for two hours and it still had a white residue clinging to the underside of a diamond. I finally found that using an electric toothbrush, the oscillating kind, not the rotary kind, helps get it off. People who expect while-you-wait appraisals aren't aware of how time-consuming it can be just to get their diamonds microscope-ready.

Preventive maintenance is the key. Regular cleaning will prevent a build-up of dirt and keep your diamonds looking like they did the first day you put them on. I suggest you invest in a home ultrasonic cleaner. They start around $30. Use it several times a week and ignore any directions about a 15 minute cleaning time. Leave the jewelry in for 45 minutes or an hour, or until it's clean. You won't hurt the diamonds.

Most difficult to get out is solid residue, perhaps fossil food, that plugs the holes underneath diamonds and accumulates in the prongs. If it's not water soluble, an ultrasonic cleaner won't get it out. I use a dental pick. You might try a toothpick or paperclip. (you won't scratch the diamond.)

If you have problems getting your diamonds clean, here's a secret formula. Make up a mixture of 1/3 water, 1/3 ammonia, and 1/3 Wisk (the laundry detergent). Seal it in a small mason jar or Tupperware container (the ammonia stinks). Soak overnight. This will soften the gunk so you can get most of it out with a toothpick. Then use the ultrasonic cleaner. Caution: don't put any jewelry with pearls, mother-of-pearl, turquoise, malachite, rhodochrosite, or other soft opaque gems in this witches' brew. You're generally safe with any transparent stone, including opal, which is mechanically, not chemically, fragile.

You should periodically have a jeweler inspect your rings and bracelets for prong wear. Some people wear down the prongs on their engagement rings in a couple of years. Others go for decades. I suppose it depends on their activities. With diamond band rings, the outside prongs on the end diamonds become worn first. With tennis bracelets, the pins holding the links adjacent to the clasp will wear through first. This happens because the links on the clasp can't move and share friction with the links on either side.

Worn prongs can be retipped or the head changed and the diamond reset. Prongs are retipped with the diamond in place. For retipping engagement rings, I use little white gold disks coated with solder on one side, designed for this purpose. For diamond jewelry set in yellow gold, I solder a gold wire to the top of the worn prong, then clip it off and file it down. This adds new metal to the top of the prong.

Platinum prongs will last much longer than white gold prongs. But they can't be retipped with platinum solder. Platinum solder melts around 2700°, which is white hot and requires welding goggles. That temperature will burn a diamond. (Burned diamonds turn white, not black.) I usually use white gold prong tips, or solder on a bit of platinum with white gold solder. A jewelry store equipped with a laser welding machine can retip platinum prongs with platinum. Laser welding machines cost $27,000. I don't have one.

Changing the head and resetting the diamond is the best fix, but this is not always feasible. Some styles of rings have heads that are integral with the body of the ring and sawing them out and fitting a new head, if it is feasible and if one can be found of the same type and proportions so as to not alter the look of the ring, is a fair reconstruction project in any case, and more so in platinum.

A wedding band worn next to an engagement ring will eventually wear a berth in it, cutting into the head at the base. Soldering the engagement ring and the wedding band together at the bottom will keep them from turning against each other and eliminate this problem. It will also solve the problem of a diamond band continually turning out of alignment with the engagement ring or will marry them into position if they don't quite fit together.

Over time, the bottom of a ring will wear thin and may bend. This is easily cured by reshanking the ring. The bottom of the ring is sawed off and a new piece of the same metal is curved, fitted, and soldered in place. But the new shank can only be as thick as the part of the old ring to which it is attached. For rings that are thin to begin with and are worn high up on the shank, reshanking might not be feasible. Also, you will lose the manufacturers markings inside the ring and any engraving when a ring is reshanked.

For enlarged or arthritic knuckles, in which case a ring made large enough to slip over the knuckle spins around on the finger, several fixes are possible. The simplest is to solder two gold balls or bars inside the shank of the ring at about the 5:00 and 7:00 positions. This grips the finger, yet the ring can still be slipped over the knuckle. This won't be enough for severely enlarged knuckles.

There are a number of types of ring shanks that open up that can be fitted to the ring. One type has a flap at the bottom of the ring that is pulled up to open the ring; another has a recessed button that is pushed with the point of a pen to release the mechanism.

I use one called a Fingermate, in which all the parts are concealed inside the diameter of the shank, showing only a thin seam where the ring opens by pulling. It opens three sizes larger than the closed position. I send the ring to the company in Florida and have them do it. I do it too infrequently to invest in the special jig they require that the jeweler have before they'll send a blank ring shank. In certain situations, such as mounting an engagement ring and wedding band on the same shank, the company requires that it be done in their factory. Anyway, that's all that they do, they've being doing it for over 40 years, and I'm sure they can do it better than I can. But this requires sending the customers' diamond rings to someone else, which the customers don't like, and it's expensive.

Never get your jewelry near mercury. It will ruin any precious metal. First, the metal becomes coated with mercury. Then the white coating of the mercury gradually disappears; it actually dissolves into the metal. Then the jewelry cracks in half. There is no cure.

20. A Diamond is Forever

Diamond has amazing physical properties. It is the hardest known substance; it may even be the hardest possible substance. Diamond will, of course, scratch glass. So will just about any other gem since glass is quite soft. So don't rely on this age-old lore for testing a diamond.

Carbon, as diamond, melts at 6422° F, the highest of any element, and diamond conducts heat more rapidly than anything else, including copper or silver (this is the property that diamond testing instruments measure). In ordinary diamonds 99% of the carbon atoms have 6 neutrons (carbon 12), with 1% of the atoms having 7 neutrons (carbon 13). Scientists have succeeded in creating pure carbon 12 and making diamonds from it. These diamonds conduct heat much better than ordinary diamonds and are used as heat sinks in advanced electronic equipment.

Diamond burns in air at 1562° F, turning into carbon dioxide[16]. However it can be heated red hot without damage (as in retipping the prongs of ring with the diamond in place) if it is coated with boric acid powder. Which melts to form a glaze that excludes air.

Diamond is unaffected by any chemicals you are likely to have in the home. Diamonds are boiled in a solution of hydrochloric and sulfuric acid to clean them after cutting. To clean a dirt-encrusted diamond, jewelers sometimes boil it in lye.

When scientists want to explore the world of ultra-high pressure they use a device called a diamond anvil cell. Two gem diamonds with the points flattened are set tip-to-tip with a metal gasket around the tip area to form a tiny chamber. The diamonds are pushed together with a simple screw, creating enormous pressure on the test materials in the chamber. Since diamonds are transparent, lasers can be shined through them to heat the specimens being tested, and observations can be made of the material in the chamber. With this bench-top device, pressures of over one million atmospheres, or 7350 tons per square inch, have been obtained.

Specially cut diamonds are used as ultrasharp scalpel blades for surgery.

Diamonds themselves can't be dated, but inclusions of other minerals, especially zircon, that formed at the same time and were incorporated in the diamond as it grew can be. Dating is done by comparing ratios of certain radioactive elements with their decay

---

16. It had been known since 1694 that diamond burns completely, leaving no ash. In 1796 English chemist Smithson Tennant discovered that diamond burns to carbon dioxide, proving that diamond is pure carbon.

products. The rate of decay is known, so the age of the diamond can be calculated. Most diamonds are about a billion years old. One rough diamond of 270 carats has been dated at 3.3 billion years, the oldest known.

The largest cut diamond in the world is the Cullinan I, a pear shape weighing 530.20 carats. It is in the king's scepter of the British crown jewels. The Cullinan diamond was found in 1905 in South Africa's Premier mine. The 3106.75 carat (1.37 lbs.) rough is thought to be itself a cleavage from a still larger stone, as yet hidden in the bosom of the earth. It was cut into 105 finished stones.

If you think the weather gets bad on earth, try it on Venus. The 1978 Pioneer Venus probe did, and survived an 865° heat wave, corrosive atmosphere, and pressure 94 times that of earth.

Peering out through a 13.5 carat diamond window, Pioneer looked at infrared radiation. The diamond window, about the size of a quarter, was cut from one of only two pieces of rough that could be found that met the specifications: free of nitrogen impurities, which would block infrared light, and internal strain. Cutting the diamond was equally difficult: the two sides had to be perfectly flat and parallel.

15 million years ago a meteor over a thousand yards across slammed into a graphite deposit in Germany creating an estimated 79,000 tons of minute diamonds. The town of Nördlingen in Bavaria is built of stone that contains millions of tiny diamonds, all less than the size of the period at the end of this sentence.

In a whimsical tour-de-force, to prove that diamond could be made from any carbon-based substance, one of the GE research team that made the first synthetic diamonds in 1954, Robert Wentorf, made diamonds from roofing tar, moth flakes, and peanut butter. (He used crunchy.)

You, like the peanut, are also a carbon-based life form (according to Mr. Spock). A company called LifeGem will turn you into a diamond after you're gone. The company will heat your specially prepared "cremains" in a vacuum at 5400° to reduce you to pure carbon, then will squeeze you into a diamond. A blue diamond. That's all they're doing now. The 18 milligrams (.09 carat) of boron in your body turns it blue. But yellow, red, and white are in the offing. You've got about 50 diamonds of various sizes in what remains of you. Cost is $22,000 per carat, with a ¼ carat minimum at $4000. A human is forever.

And you don't have to spend forever without your best friend. Rover can join you when his time comes. The company reports that half its business is for pets.

21. The Other Side Of The Counter

The customer is always right, right? Well, here's some lessons on how to be more right.

"Can you do any better?" In my store the answer is no. I put the real prices on the jewelry to begin with. If you're a heavy buyer or hit on something I've been staring at for too long, I'll offer a little bit off. Many items are already quietly marked down. So don't ask.

Other stores do it differently. A friend if mine gives 20% off on everything to everybody. You don't have to ask, he offers. Of course, he adds the discount to the price to begin with. If the store has a policy of giving discounts only to those who ask, it's unfair to the silent majority who are uncomfortable with bargaining and just want a fair price. Anyhow, they're probably charging too much even with the discount. Go someplace else.

"No sales tax for cash?" Don't ask. Here's an article I wrote in one of the newsletters I send to my customers.

> The state of New Jersey charges you sales tax. Unfortunately, it makes me collect it from you. I'm often asked if the sales tax goes away if the customer pays cash. It does not.
>
> Such a customer is either asking for a 6% discount for the convenience of cash or, worse, suborning the crime of tax evasion by asking me to do the sale off the books.
>
> Cash is convenient, not magical. Just about all the money, in whatever form, is deposited in the bank so I can write the checks to pay my bills. Just about all the merchandise is shipped to the store and paid for by check. I also give myself a paycheck (I would like to collect Social Security some day.)
>
> The advantages of cash are same day clearance at the bank, saving the 1.5-3% a charge costs me, and, of course, cash doesn't bounce.
>
> Sure, I like cash. But not enough to give 2 to 4 times the charge fee off. Besides, if I were going to cheat on your taxes, I sure wouldn't tell you about it.
>
> Cheer up! Taxes are better than that other thing you can't avoid.

"How do I know it's real?" How do I know your money isn't counterfeit?

"Be honest!" When was the last time you beat your wife/abused your child?

"How do I know I'll get the same diamond back?" You don't.

Have you hugged your jeweler today?

Merchants sign an agreement with charge card companies that forbids stating a preference for one card over another or charging extra for charge cards. Merchant charge card fees, which are percentages of the total amount of the transaction, including sales tax, add up – a few thousand dollars a year. That's OK. It's a cost of doing business. But on that diamond sale with 15-20% profit, a charge card fee can take from 8% to 22% of that, depending on the card. I can't tell you officially which card the merchant loves to hate, but, if the cards were listed alphabetically, it would come first.

People hate to leave their diamonds. I even had one customer who wanted an evaluation of her diamond ring, but wouldn't take it off her finger. I hear so many stories of switched diamonds that it's impossible for even a fraction of them to be true. Sharp practice is one thing, felony theft is another. How many in your profession are criminals? Are you? If you feel uneasy about a particular store, say a polite good-bye and go somewhere else. If you feel uneasy about every store, you've got a problem. You have to trust someone, sometime.

Well, we've had an amusing time discussing all those other people. I'll sum up with **Joseph's Three Laws of Retail Dynamics** and then a story.

The Law of Inverse Anxiety
The smaller the diamond, the bigger the worry about leaving it.

The Law of Least Favorable Assumption
Wherever it was fixed, that's where it broke again.

The Law of Inappropriate Negotiation
The smaller the price, the harder the bargaining.

A Diamond As Big As The Ritz
I have a sign in my window saying "The Ideal Cut Diamond Sold Here." Next to the sign is a 3 inch prop diamond in a box and a copy of the previous edition of this book with another sign that says "Diamond Mistake Insurance, $6.95"

One day, an elderly gentleman came in and inquired as to the price of the ideal cut diamond in the window. He was crestfallen after I gently explained that it wasn't a real diamond.

Another time, I saw two people outside the window animatedly talking and pointing at the "diamond". They came in, a grandmother with her teen-age grandson. The grandson just couldn't wait to find out if that big diamond was really $6.95. I patiently explained to him that it wasn't a real diamond. "See", the grandmother chided him, "The $6.95 is for the insurance".

Appendix A. Precious Metals

24 karat gold is pure gold. Pure gold is too soft for jewelry use and so it is alloyed with other metals to improve its hardness. 14 karat gold is 14/24ths or 58.3% gold. Likewise, 18 karat gold is 75% gold and 10 karat gold is 41.7% gold. That is why you will sometimes see gold jewelry stamped with numbers: 585 means 14k and 750 means 18k. (Italian14k is stamped 585 instead of 583 because their law requires the extra tiny bit of gold.)

Mark	Karat	Typical Origin
333	8	Germany
375	9	England, Ireland
417	10	U.S.
583/585	14	U.S, Russia
750	18	Most of World
875	21	Middle East
917	22	India
999	24	China, S.E. Asia

Silver is also marked with a number indicating its fineness, or percentage of pure silver. This is why you will commonly see sterling silver marked 925. (Although the term "sterling" has connotations of superiority or excellence, the only thing it means in this context is that the metal is 92.5% silver.) You may also see silver marked 800 (Germany), 830 (Scandanavia), or 900 (coin silver). "Nickel silver" and "German silver" contain no silver.

Gold-filled jewelry is marked 1/20 12k, 1/20 14k, 1/10 10k RGP (rolled gold plate), etc. This means that a thin layer of gold of the designated karatage is bonded to base metal such that the weight of the gold will be 1/20th, etc. of the weight of the finished article. The layer of gold on gold-filled jewelry is much thicker than on gold-plated jewelry and so will last a much longer time. Watch out for jewelry stamped 18k HGE. HGE means Heavy Gold Electroplate, which basically means junk.

An irony of our culture is that high karat gold, 21, 22, or 24 karat is spurned as cheap-looking for its orangy-yellow color. The gold-plated trinkets we see everywhere are covered with a thin (10-100 millionths of an inch) layer of pure gold and so we associate the color of pure gold with the fake and the pale color of 14k with the real. Other cultures perceive these colors of gold in just the reverse.

14 or 18 karat yellow gold has copper and silver added to the pure gold. Pink gold is created by adding just copper and white gold by adding copper and nickel. Nickel white gold is subject to attack from chlorine compounds so it is advisable to have the head (prongs) of an engagement ring made from platinum.

You may have noticed that gold chains seem to come in a variety of colors, from pale yellow to too yellow. This is because most gold chains are gold-plated over the gold to give the chain, the lock, and the solder a uniform color. Manufacturers, strive for a color called "Hamilton gold", which is too yellow for American tastes. Why manufacturers, especially the Italians, make gold chains a color their customers dislike is a question for someone wiser than me, since gold-plating can be done in any shade.

When the Spanish conquistadors arrived in South America, they found the Indians ingeniously working small grains of platinum found in stream beds.

Because of its high melting point, over 3000°, the Spanish couldn't do much with it and they named it *platina*, a derogatory meaning "little silver".

Platinum came into its own in the early 20th century in Edwardian and Art Deco jewelry. In 1942, the U.S. Government declared Platinum a strategic metal and white gold was substituted until after the war

Unlike white gold, platinum has no springiness, so prongs can be laid completely against a stone or diamond with ease. Even when prongs are worn thin, they still hold. Platinum is also completely inert and immune to any kind of corrosion.

Pure platinum is too soft for jewelry, so its alloyed with other metals in the same family, usually iridium or ruthenium, or, lately, cobalt (it casts better, but makes the alloy slightly magnetic). Platinum jewelry will be stamped *90% platinum 10% iridium, 95% platinum 5% ruthenium,* or *950 platinum* or just *platinum*. The latter two will usually be platinum/cobalt. If jewelry is just stamped platinum, it must be at least 95% pure.

Remember way back to 1906? I don't either. That's when the law governing marking of precious metals was enacted. It's called the National Gold And Silver Marking Act.

The act was amended a few times, for example to allow trade organizations the right to sue violators. The latest amendment was in 1976, taking effect in 1981. This amendment tightened up the tolerances for gold alloys, such as 14 karat. The original act allowed 13 1/2 karat to be marked 14 karat if the article contained no solder, and allowed 13 karat to be so marked if it did.

This was because assay techniques weren't as good in those days and low karat solder was used, which would lower the karat of the piece as a whole. (This is why old pieces have black areas around the solder joints where the low karat solder has tarnished.) Modern assays can determine the karat of gold to parts per million and modern solders, called plumb solders, are the same karat as the gold,using advanced alloys to lower the melting point rather than simply lowering the gold content. There has recently come on the market a patented plumb platinum solder. Previously the highest platinum content for solder was 20%. This is why you may see a gray line where your platinum ring was soldered.

The tolerances now are 3 parts per thousand for pieces containing no solder and 7 parts per thousand for pieces containing solder. This is called plumb gold. (Odd that a word meaning lead should describe the purity of gold.) In the early 1980's with the so-called "plumb law" newly in effect, manufacturers would stamp a "P" after the quality mark, i.e., "14KP", the "P" standing for plumb. This practice has been discontinued.

The act does not require that jewelry be stamped with a quality mark (i.e. 14k). However it does require that, if something is quality marked, it must also be trademarked with the registered symbol of the manufacturer. This is not always done. If the jewelry is custom made by a jeweler, I wouldn't be concerned about it. Mom and pop stores don't usually register trademarks, and some pieces can be difficult to stamp. But anything made by a factory should definitely be both quality marked and trademarked.

Precious metals are weighed in troy ounces. A troy ounce is about 10% larger than the avoirdupois ounce that you are familiar with. The troy weight system is named after Troyes, France, where it was developed way back when. A troy ounce is divided into 20 penny-weights, abbreviated dwt. There are 12 troy ounces to a troy pound.

Grams are also a commonly used weight for jewelry. Grams are a metric system unit of weight. Grams are usually used for gold chains, charms, and earrings. Pennyweights are still used for ring castings and for scrap gold. There are 31.1 grams in a troy ounce and 28.35 grams in an avoirdupois ounce. A kilogram is 1000 grams, or 2.2 pounds. A pound is 454 grams.

Appendix B. Gemology

Gemology is more than diamonds. The following article I wrote in one of my newsletters in 1997 should give you a feel for what gemology is about.

How Do They Do That? – Gem Identification

Most people think that the color makes the gem. Actually, the colors of most gems are accidental, caused by trace amounts of impurities, usually metals, in the crystal. That's how there can be a dark green garnet or tourmaline that you think is an emerald. It's the chemical and physical make-up that determines what anything is, including gems.

Color is a starting point for the gemologist – it narrows down the possibilities. Other observations give further clues. I always check the brilliance. A too-bright stone that resembles amethyst would have me checking for synthetic sapphire, a common substitute.

Under the microscope certain gems have distinctive features. Seeing double images of the back facets (looking through the top of the stone) rules out certain classes of crystals and thus certain gems. Zircon and peridot have this doubling in spades. Some peridots also have distinctive inclusions called "lily-pads" and some red garnets have fine needles that cross each other at certain angles. Diamonds sometimes have "naturals", part of the surface of the rough diamond that was not cut away, that are distinctive. Both diamonds and black onyx have a distinctive fracture or chip. Gas bubbles almost always mean a synthetic stone. And the most common type of synthetic ruby has curved bands inside.

An instrument called a polariscope enables the gemologist to shine polarized light through the stone. Ordinary light is like a wheel with spokes. Each spoke is a differently oriented light ray. A polarizer is like a venetian blind, it only lets in the spokes parallel to the slats. Polaroid sunglasses have the "slats" running up and down to block light that has become polarized by being reflected from horizontal surfaces and so cut down glare.

When a gem is viewed in polarized light, magical things happen. Some blink light and dark as they are rotated, some stay dark, and some stay light. With some stones a rainbow will appear at one spot which becomes a colored bulls-eye when magnified. This is called an optic figure. Glass and plastic have snake-like bands which become a cross when the stone is rotated. (your optician knows all about this). Synthetic spinel has a diagnostic cross-hatch pattern. Blue topaz has a bulls-eye with a line through it and aquamarine has a bulls-eye with a cross. Quartz has its own kind of bulls-eye. These patterns derive from the atomic structure of the material.

The refractive index of a gem is a measure of its ability to bend light. An instrument called a refractometer can precisely measure refractive index. A gem is placed on the glass of the instrument with a drop of contact liquid and light is reflected off of it and onto a scale. The more brilliant the gem the higher up the scale the light is reflected. Aquamarine reads about 1.58, blue topaz 1.62, synthetic spinel 1.73, and zircon doesn't read at all – its refractive index is above the limits of the instrument. These are very different results and easily separate these four light blue stones.

Ultraviolet light is also a useful tool. Some gems fluoresce, that is, glow various colors. Many synthetics and glass light up while their natural counterparts do not.

Other instruments include a spectroscope, in which light shined through the gem is spread out by a prism. Some gems show dark lines or bands where certain elements in their atomic structure have absorbed certain colors of light, a dichroscope that shows if the stone has different colors when observed from different directions, proof of double refraction (see page 64), and a Chelsea filter, a dark red lens, through which certain green gems appear red.

The following through-the-microscope photos show classic gemological characteristics that are used to identify gemstones.

This Photo of a peridot clearly shows double images of the back facets and proves double refraction.

Fig. 66

These colorless curved lines, called striae, are throughout the stone. This is proof that this sapphire imitation alexandrite is man-made. They are caused by a rotating manufacturing process.

Fig. 67

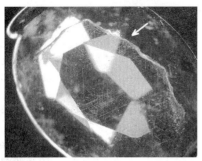

Fig. 68

Fig. 69

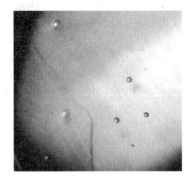

Fig. 70

Fig. 71

The three photos top and right are of a garnet and glass doublet, a stone that was often used to imitate other gems before the advent of modern synthetics. I still see them in old jewelry that customers bring in.

Garnet is the only gemstone that will fuse directly to glass, without glue. The garnet top gives this imitation higher luster and more durability than glass. Even though the garnet is red, it's only a thin sliver and the stone takes on the color of the glass, which can be any color. Usually the garnet covers just the table of the stone, not the whole crown. In the top left photo, the arrow points to the ragged border of the garnet slice.

What makes this photo so interesting are the classic needle inclusions in the garnet, shown in the close-up at top right. This little bit of garnet exhibits a profusion of oriented needles that are diagnostic for red garnet. The needles are of a mineral called rutile that formed inside the garnet and lined up with its crystal structure. Needles in the same plane cross each other at 70° and 110°.

Also present are a lot of gas bubbles, as seen in the lower right photo, formed by trapped air in the fusion plane between the garnet and the glass.

Gas bubbles always indicate some sort of fakery; they do not occur in natural gems, other than amber and the volcanic glass obsidian. So this garnet and glass doublet shows the real and the fake together. The left bottom photo shows gas bubbles very clearly. You can even see the shadows of the bubbles. It's a photo of a stone with a glass dome covering a thin iridescent layer on the bottom. The gas bubbles are in the glass. It's attractive, with a vague resemblance to opal, but It really doesn't look like any natural gem.